Sport, Forced Migration, and the 'Refugee Crisis'

Drawing on original research, this book looks at what sport can tell us about the social processes, patterns, and outcomes of forced migration and the 'refugee crisis'.

Adopting a systems theory framework and examining different sport disciplines, performance levels, and settings, it represents a significant contribution to our understanding of one of the most urgent social issues facing the modern world. The book explores four key aspects of sport's intersection with forced migration. Firstly, it looks at how the media covers sport in relation to the 'refugee crisis', specifically coverage of refugee elite athletes. Secondly, it examines the adaptation of sport organisations to the 'refugee crisis', including the culture, programmes, and structures that promote or obstruct sport for and with refugees. Thirdly, the book looks at sport in refugee sites, and how sport can be used as therapy, an escape, or empowerment for refugees but also how it can reinforce the divisions between staff and the refugees themselves. Finally, the book looks at how forced migration influences and is influenced by participation in elite sport, by examining the biographies of elite refugee athletes.

A richly descriptive, critical, and illuminating piece of work, this book is fascinating reading for anybody with an interest in sport, migration, sociology, or the relationship between sport and wider society.

Enrico Michelini is Professor of sociology and economy of sport at the University of Saarland, Germany. His research focuses on sport in the contexts of health promotion, human migration, and social conflicts. In his projects, he has worked with different qualitative methods and particularly with document analysis, ethnography, and interviews. His current research focus concerns the role of sport in the context of the so-called 'refugee crisis'.

Routledge Focus on Sport, Culture, and Society

Routledge Focus on Sport, Culture, and Society showcases the latest cutting-edge research in the sociology of sport and exercise. Concise in form (20,000–50,000 words) and published quickly (within three months), the books in this series represent an important channel through which authors can disseminate their research swiftly and make an impact on current debates. We welcome submissions on any topic within the sociocultural study of sport and exercise, including but not limited to subjects such as gender, race, sexuality, disability, politics, the media, social theory, Olympic Studies, and the ethics and philosophy of sport. The series aims to be theoretically informed, empirically grounded, and international in reach, and will include a diversity of methodological approaches.

Available in this series:

Racism and English Football
For Club and Country
Daniel Burdsey

Referees, Match Officials and Abuse
Research and Implications for Policy
Tom Webb, Mike Rayner, Jamie Cleland and Jimmy O'Gorman

On Boxing
Critical Interventions in the Bittersweet Science
Joseph D Lewandowski

Sport, Forced Migration and the 'Refugee Crisis'
Enrico Michelini

For more information about this series, please visit: https://www.routledge.com/Routledge-Focus-on-Sport-Culture-and-Society/book-series/RFSCS

Sport, Forced Migration, and the 'Refugee Crisis'

Enrico Michelini

First published 2023
by Routledge
4 Park Square, Milton Park, Abingdon, Oxon OX14 4RN

and by Routledge
605 Third Avenue, New York, NY 10158

Routledge is an imprint of the Taylor & Francis Group, an informa business

© 2023 Enrico Michelini

The right of Enrico Michelini to be identified as author of this work has been asserted in accordance with sections 77 and 78 of the Copyright, Designs and Patents Act 1988.

The Open Access version of this book, available at www.taylorfrancis.com, has been made available under a Creative Commons Attribution 4.0 license.

Trademark notice: Product or corporate names may be trademarks or registered trademarks, and are used only for identification and explanation without intent to infringe.

British Library Cataloguing-in-Publication Data
A catalogue record for this book is available from the British Library

ISBN: 978-1-032-44141-2 (hbk)
ISBN: 978-1-032-44143-6 (pbk)
ISBN: 978-1-003-37067-3 (ebk)

DOI: 10.4324/9781003370673

Typeset in Times New Roman
by MPS Limited, Dehradun

This book is dedicated to refugees all over the world.

Contents

List of Figures x
List of Tables xi
Preface xii
Acknowledgements xvi
List of Abbreviations xvii

1 Introduction 1

   1.1 Sport and the 'refugee crisis' as a research topic 2
   1.2 Research question 4
   1.3 Structure 5

2 State of the Art Research on Forced Migration and Sport 7

   2.1 Neighbouring disciplines and research areas 7
   2.2 Knowledge on forced migration and sport 10
   2.3 Critical review of the literature 12

3 Definitions of Key Terms in Forced Migration and Sport 14

   3.1 Migrant, displaced person, and refugee 14
   3.2 Physical activity, exercise, and sport 16
   3.3 Crisis and migration crises 17

4 The 'Refugee Crisis' — 20

4.1 The context of the 'refugee crisis' 20
4.2 The 'refugee crisis' as a process 24
4.3 Sport in the 'refugee crisis' 26

5 Systems Theoretical Framework — 27

5.1 Systems theory 28
    5.1.1 General assumptions 28
    5.1.2 Specific concepts 30
    5.1.3 Typification of the considered systems 34
5.2 Other theories 37

6 Methodical Approaches of the Projects — 39

6.1 Researching mass media 41
6.2 Researching sport organisations 43
6.3 Researching refugee sites 44
6.4 Researching refugee athletes 46

7 Results of the Projects — 50

7.1 Sport and forced migration in the mass media 50
7.2 Activities for refugees in sports clubs 54
7.3 Physical activity in refugee sites 58
7.4 Forced migration and elite sport 62

8 Overarching Discussion of the Results — 68

8.1 Representations of refugee athletes 68
8.2 Organisations and sport activities for refugees 71
8.3 Holistic considerations of the research 73

9 Conclusion 77

9.1 The role of sport within the 'refugee crisis' 78
    9.1.1 Elite sport 79
    9.1.2 Amateur sport 81
    9.1.3 Leisure sport 83
9.2 Limitations 85
    9.2.1 Methodological aspects 86
    9.2.2 Practical aspects 87
9.3 Future perspectives 88
    9.3.1 Research gaps 88
    9.3.2 Future scientific agenda 90
    9.3.3 Call to the scientific community 91

Articles by the Author 93
References 95
Index 122

Figures

3.1	A typology of migrants	15
4.1	Timeline of the European 'refugee crisis'	22
4.2	Asylum applications in Europe between 2013 and 2018 (UNHCR, 2022a)	24
5.1	A typology of systems	29
6.1	Selection of relevant articles	42
7.1	Asylum applications and articles in Germany	52
7.2	Impact of the 'refugee crisis' on sports clubs	55
7.3	Dynamic understanding of time	64
8.1	Research projects and types of systems	69
9.1	Fields of sport and phases of the 'refugee crisis'	79

Tables

1.1	Research questions	5
5.1	Sociological theories applied in the research	27
6.1	Methodological approaches of the habilitation	40
6.2	Distribution of articles on *forced migration and sport*	42
6.3	Catalogue of interviews in sports clubs	44
6.4	Catalogue of interviews in Niamey's refugee sites	45
6.5	Sample of *forced migration and elite sport*	47
7.1	Research projects and scientific articles	51
7.2	Distribution of articles per year and category	53
7.3	Conditions for refugee-specific sport programmes	56
8.1	Sport for refugees in sports clubs and refugee sites	72
8.2	Consideration of the four projects	74

Preface

This preface aims to contextualise the present version of the book in the changed social context in 2022, with particular reference to the COVID-19 pandemic and the Russia-Ukraine war. My research work on forced migration and sport started in 2015, shortly before the height of the so-called 'European refugee crisis'. The research projects included in this manuscript were concluded before 2020, i.e. before the outbreak of the COVID-19 pandemic. The first unpublished version of this book was submitted as one of the requirements of my habilitation at the Humboldt University of Berlin in May 2021. This means that more than one year has passed between the first unpublished version and this printed one.

This version has been revised but not updated. That is, I incorporated the feedback of different reviewers to improve the manuscript's readability and to address specific critiques, but neither was the stand of the research nor that of my research projects and the societal context. This preface is an effort to remedy these shortcomings.

As regards the state of research, some important publications have been issued since finalising this work. Among others, De Martini Ugolotti and Caudwell (2021) and the special issue on Sport in Society on Forced Migration and Sport edited by Spaaij, Luguetti, and De Martini Ugolotti (2021) are particularly significant. This should not, however, lead to an overestimation of the scientific discussion's fervency around this topic in recent years. Instead, it is more likely that the publications are the outcomes of projects that began when the 'refugee crisis' was a leading socio-political concern. The COVID-19 pandemic decreased the relevance of this topic and the possibility to study it, despite the fact that the situation of refugees around the world has deteriorated severely. The Russia-Ukraine conflict and the resultant

Preface xiii

new 'refugee crisis' might reignite the conversation about forced migration and sport.

The pandemic represented a major obstacle also for my research work. Hence, from 2020, I focused on analysing and interpreting the previously collected data and on publishing other works based on my material (Burdsey, Michelini, & Agergaard, 2022; Michelini, Quade, Burrmann, & Neuber, 2021; Michelini & Schreiner, 2022-Submitted; Michelini & Seiberth, 2022). The only notable exception is a project involving football players with a refugee background, which I carried out in cooperation with the Egidius Braun Foundation (Michelini, Bruland, & Janning, 2022). After a break of over three years due to the corona pandemic, a follow-up study at Niamey's refugee sites was planned for summer 2022.

Finally, the change in societal context since mid-2021 must be addressed. Against the background of the Russia-Ukraine war, I feel compelled to look at my research and reflect on its implications in view of the current situation. The conflicts in Syria and Ukraine cannot be compared with one another, yet they both caused 'refugee crises' in Europe. According to UNHCR (2022b), 6.7 million refugees fled Syria, with one million currently residing in Europe. Within three months of the outbreak of the conflict in Ukraine, nearly 5.5 million Ukrainians left the country (UNHCR, 2022c). While Eastern Europe—particularly Poland—is hosting the majority of Ukrainian refugees, European countries have been managing the flow of migration through the redistribution of refugees across countries.

In the early phase of the Ukraine war, heated discussions arose about the racial disparity in the media between Syrian and Ukrainian refugees. I fully agree with the critics. This comparison visibly exposed the eradication of racial humanitarianism. The first wave of (Syrian) refugees was welcomed with much solidarity by parts of the European population. Yet the general attitude towards refugees deteriorated following a series of events (e.g. attacks in Paris and assaults in Cologne on New Year's Eve). Yet I feel reassured by the solidarity and enthusiasm for Ukrainian refugees I am currently witnessing, and hope this positive attitude will persist in the time to come. I also hope that other humanitarian crises around the world will not be forgotten.

I argue in this book that 'refugee crises' are (total) phenomena that are socially constructed, highly politicised and have an impact on society as a whole; they also have an impact on sport. Sport functioned as a stage during the 2015 'European refugee crisis' where both empathy and hostility were on full display. I will demonstrate that the sport system's response to this event was 'sensible' at different levels. It is too early to analyse the sport system's response to the 'Ukrainian refugee crisis' (which has indeed already become an accepted designation), but in the early phase of the conflict, athletes have already been using sport to express either dissent or assent; sport facilities have again become emergency shelters for displaced persons; and the first fundraisers were organised by sport organisations.

This book presents the results of four research projects, which targeted different aspects of the role of sport in the context of the 'refugee crisis': (1) mass media; (2) sport organisations; (3) refugee sites; and (4) athletes with a refugee background. Without raising too much anticipation, if you read this book, you might agree with me that:

1   There are many reasons for being critical of the mass media's reports on the 'refugee crisis'. Scandalmongering, humoral, and even racist features were evident. We will hopefully see more unbiased journalism during the 'Ukrainian refugee crisis'.
2   Sports clubs were very active and learned a lot during the 'refugee crisis'. This know-how is ready to be re-activated in the case of Ukrainian refugees. It is possible, however, that the rapid succession of 'crises' may have a de-sensitising effect.
3   It is a disgrace that refugee sites exist and become long-term settlements. Any effort to alleviate the burden of the residents is valuable. Yet, the expectations of sport in this context are immense and largely overestimated.
4   Athletes with a refugee background face tremendous pressure and should get more support in their engagement in sport activities after migrating. There is still much work to do to sensitise sport organisations, athletes, and coaches.

Agamben (Agamben, 1998) speaks of refugees as a 'nomos of our time' because they expose our political system's profound contradictions and injustice. If 'refugee crises' are rapidly recurring phenomena, which are perceived as a new emergency, their management will always be perceived as being critical in repeated and accelerating cycles.

Until a systemic solution is found, unbiased journalism, social activism, civic education, and (critical) research are important means of opinion formation. I hope that these discourses—with a small contribution by this book—can maintain a high level of attention on the dramatic situation of refugees all over the world—not only that of Ukrainians, but also of those affected by other existing but ignored humanitarian crises. Indeed and despite this basic human right is often denied, 'Everyone has the right to seek and to enjoy in other countries asylum from persecution' (UN, 1948, Article 14).

Acknowledgements

I owe sincere gratitude to many people and organisations for generously supporting this research. The participation of many refugee athletes (in particular, Moayad 'Mo' Al Hammal) and sports club volunteers was fundamental for data collection. UNHCR facilitated the work in refugee sites in Niamey. Alessandra Morelli, Giulia Raffaelli, and, last but not least, Marzia Vigliaroni provided invaluable support in organising and conducting research in Niger. Robert Junior Thea and Abarchi El Massaoud were essential in introducing me to the sites. The student assistants Birte Krause, Jörn Schäfer, and Jennifer Bruland significantly contributed to the research carried out for this book. Several friends and colleagues, amongst others Felix Kühnle, Benjamin Zander, and Jennifer Schmitz, who did not have a vested interest in this work, gave me useful feedback. My family was extremely patient and understanding of my workaholism. Moreover, the Institute of Sport and Sport Science of the TU Dortmund supported part of my research initiatives and travels. Finally, I would like to extend sincere thanks to my reviewers and advisors, particularly Ulrike Burrmann, who substantially counselled and supported me in this effort for seven long years.

This book is a revised version of the thesis submitted by the author in 2021 for the acquisition of the habilitation degree at the Faculty of Sport and Arts of the HU Berlin.

List of Abbreviations*

BJ	Bakery Jatta
CP	Contact person
DFB	German Football Association
DOSB	German Olympic Sports Federation
dsj	Youth section of the German Olympic Sports Federation
IDP	Internally-displaced person
IOC	International Olympic Committee
NOC	National Olympic Committee
NGO	Non-governmental organisation
OtS	Orientation through Sport
PA	Physical Activity
ROT	Refugee Olympic Team
SFDP	Sport for Development and Peace
TU Dortmund	Technical University of Dortmund
UN	United Nations
UNHCR	United Nations High Commissioner for Refugees
WHO	World Health Organization
YM	Yusra Mardini

* These terms are only abbreviated when their repetition unnecessarily slows down the reading of the document and when they do not add depth to the text.

1 Introduction

The tabloid newspaper *Bild* portrayed the rise of Bakery Jatta as a professional football player with almost fan-alike admiration. The word 'fairy tale' was widely used to describe the sport career of this young Gambian, who migrated to Europe in 2015 in the context of the 'refugee crisis' and rapidly made a name for himself in one of the world's top football leagues. Within just a few years, that same newspaper initiated and pushed a media campaign depicting Jatta as an impostor.

In 2016, over 30 young asylum seekers joined a small and traditional sports club in the suburb of a large German city. When these new members joined, the club experienced numerous changes, renewed itself and mobilised additional resources. At their request, the club's first cricket team was established in 2017 and joined the German cricket league. Despite its successes and the generous involvement of dozens of participants, the cricket team dealt with social conflicts between internal factions and part of the players were recruited by other cricket teams, resulting in the dropout of some team members.

In *Hamdallaye*, a refugee site in the capital city of Niger, sport activities take place regularly despite discouraging conditions. In cooperation with the Fondazione Milan, the site's management organises, offers, and promotes a variety of sport disciplines, predominantly football. In this particular setting, sport is understood as a therapy that can help refugees who were evacuated from Libya to Niger to recover from their traumatic experiences.

Several Syrian elite water polo players migrated to Europe following the outbreak of the Syrian Civil War. After resettling in different countries and resuming their sport careers, they participated in various water polo events as one team. While they agree that sport helped them integrate in Europe, their biographical trajectories differ significantly. Only one of the several young talents who were once teammates still plays water polo at a professional level.

DOI: 10.4324/9781003370673-1

2 *Introduction*

These anecdotes exemplify some of the potential roles sport has played in the context of the 'refugee crisis'. Using a sociological approach, this book explores what lies behind the allegedly close relationship between the 'refugee crisis' and the sport system. This chapter sheds light on the approach taken to explain this social phenomenon, to further elaborate the leading research questions and to outline the main features of this book.

1.1 Sport and the 'refugee crisis' as a research topic

Many migrants arrived in the European Union (EU) via the Mediterranean Sea or overland through Southeast Europe between 2013 and 2018. The majority were Syrians, Iraqis, and Afghans escaping countries riddled by ongoing armed conflict (UNHCR, 2021). Asylum applications in Europe increased considerably between 2015 and 2016 (Eurostat, 2020).

The often politicised expression 'refugee crisis' (Sigona, 2018)[1] was coined to describe this massive displacement of people from West Asia and North Africa to the EU, and evolved to become a total social fact (Mauss, 2002), with economic, legal, political, and religious implications. Economically, the crisis required the development of expensive management programmes and challenged European governments' financial resources (Kancs & Lecca, 2018). Juridically, asylum legislation became subject to a 'recast exercise' (Trauner, 2016). Politically, the inability to agree on a collective approach nearly caused the collapse of the EU, partly as a consequence of the rise of populist and anti-immigrant parties (Algan et al., 2017). Religiously, the crisis revived interreligious rivalries and aroused islamophobia (Schmiedel & Smith, 2018).

Following the 'long summer of migration' in 2015, many European countries were engaged in controversial political debates about the social integration of refugees. These discussions also included the role of sport, which is often considered an engine of integration (Council of Europe, 2020; European Commission, 2007; German Federal Government, 2007).

The positive values of sport as a tool for promoting human rights, encouraging peace, and fostering international understanding in a spirit of mutual respect between people can be seen to play an important role in helping both host societies and new arrivals in a community come together to build new social connections. Common interests and values can be shared through sport, bringing people together to promote intercultural dialogue, overcome differences, and reduce intolerance.

(Council of Europe, 2020, online document)

These assumptions were considered self-evident long before the 'refugee crisis' emerged and have been continuously echoed, amongst others, by the mass media and by the sport system itself. However, a large part of the sociological community agrees that a univocal positive view of the impact of sport is distorted and romanticised (Coalter, 2008; Dowling, 2020; Hoberman, 2011). Guided by a 'suspicious attitude', this work neither intends to praise nor blame sport in the context of forced migration, and instead to conduct an in-depth and balanced analysis of its many facets. Indeed, the relationship between the 'refugee crisis' and the sport system is not limited to the abstract political discussion on integration and involves—amongst other aspects—the mass media's representation of refugees in sport, sports clubs' adaptation processes, the creation of sport offers for refugees in reception sites, and the inclusion of refugee elite athletes in sport. Exploring these topics yields some beautiful fairy tales and awful nightmares and exposes the deep contradictions in modern society.

The state of research, the definitions of key terms and leading concepts from broader discussions on sport and migration sociologies represent the scientific pillar of this book. By explicitly focussing on social patterns concerning refugees and sport in the midst of the 'refugee crisis', this book draws heavily on the sociological discussion of forced migration and sport (Michelini, 2020b; Middleton et al., 2020; Spaaij et al., 2019). To answer the research question 'What role does sport play in the context of the "refugee crisis"?' with a satisfying degree of completeness and multi-facetedness, this book builds on distinct research lines developed in different projects:

- The first project explores how the topic *forced migration and sport* was covered in the press. This topic is examined on the basis of a catalogue of German newspaper articles.
- The second project reviews the adaptations German sports clubs introduced during the 'refugee crisis'. Various empirical approaches are used to analyse sports clubs that provided sport offers for refugees.

4 Introduction

- The third project considers sport in the setting of refugee sites. An ethnographic research study was carried out by taking part in different sport activities offered in the refugee sites of Niamey (Niger).
- In the fourth project, the sport careers of young athletes with a refugee background are examined longitudinally based on a sample of (former) elite Syrian water polo players, who sought asylum in different European countries.

This book explores the role of sport in the context of the 'refugee crisis' based on these four projects, which differ in terms of their underlying research questions, theoretical frameworks (Luhmann's systems theory, Hurrelmann's socialisation theory and Foucault's discourse analysis) and empirical methodologies (interviews, ethnography, document analysis). While the projects focus mostly on the German case, they also shed some light on the European and global aspects of this topic. The overarching consideration of this topic through a systems theoretical framework enables a differentiated analysis of its various aspects under both a descriptive and critical perspective. With its generality claim, this theory is believed to have the potential to successfully examine, relate, and contextualise this heterogeneous content.

1.2 Research question

The leading research question of this book is 'What role does sport play in the context of the "refugee crisis"?' Specific sub-questions guided the four projects conducted on this topic. Within the scope of the four projects, selected aspects were favoured over others and considered in separate articles, which were published earlier and constitute the backbone of this book. Importantly, a cumulative habilitation requires the researcher to first focus on publishing scientific journal articles. The overarching questions addressed by both the research projects and this book were deferred until a later phase of the research process and were in part newly conceived and assessed during the writing process of this manuscript.

The sub-questions presented in Table 1.1 were partly assessed through the journal articles attached to this book, and represent the starting point for solving the fragmented research 'puzzle' (Eckstein, 1975, p. 91). This is achieved through two consecutive parts. First, the main part of this text addresses the sub-questions connected to each project by considering the findings of the published articles and

Table 1.1 Research questions

Main Question	Projects' Questions	Examples of Sub-questions
What role does sport play in the context of the 'refugee crisis'?	How does the mass media represent sport in the context of the 'refugee crisis'?	Which topics emerge from newspaper articles' representation of sport in the context of the 'refugee crisis'? How do newspaper articles represent refugee athletes in the context of the 'refugee crisis'?
	How do sports clubs organise sport activities for refugees?	How did sports clubs adapt to the 'refugee crisis'? Which conditions promote or prevent the creation of activities for refugees in sports clubs?
	How do refugee sites organise sport activities for refugees?	What role does organised sport play in refugee sites? What does sport mean for residents of refugee sites?
	How do migration and sport experiences influence the biographies of refugee athletes?	What characterises the sport careers of refugee athletes? What role does sport play for athletes after forced migration?

of additional unpublished material, which already existed or was created for this book. Second, the discussion chapter merges and connects the results of the individual projects and answers the main research question.

1.3 Structure

The nine chapters of this book serve to exhaustively outline the author's research work on the topic *forced migration and sport*, based in particular on the four projects mentioned above. Before delving further into these projects, the reader can find all relevant information on the state of research (Chapter 2), the definitions of terms (Chapter 3), the topic's overall social context (Chapter 4) and the description of the theoretical framework (Chapter 5). Following the explanation of the empirical approach (Chapter 6), the reader will be guided by an overarching red line based on the four individual projects and their main results (Chapter 7). This book then discusses the four projects within a single comprehensive research programme on *forced migration and sport* (Chapter 8), and ends with a conclusion (Chapter 9), which reviews the main research question. A critical reflection on the research carried out within the scope of this study, the identification of gaps and a proposal for a future research agenda conclude this book.

Note

1 A critical, in-depth investigation of the term 'refugee crisis' and other related terminology is contained in Chapters 3 and 4.

2 State of the Art Research on Forced Migration and Sport

This chapter reviews the general state of research on the topic *forced migration and sport*. It elaborates the position of the present book within the broader scientific context and relevant sociological research programmes. By describing the current knowledge about the topic being studied, a comprehensive overview of what has already been done in the field and what needs further investigation are provided. After locating this study within neighbouring disciplines, three systematic literature reviews on the topic *forced migration and sport* are presented. A critical reflection on the state of research concludes this chapter.

2.1 Neighbouring disciplines and research areas

This research is positioned between what Kneer and Schroer (2010) call two types of 'special sociologies': the sociology of migration and the sociology of sport.

The sociology of migration aims to understand migration patterns and processes from a social perspective (Pries, 2010). Traditionally, it has focused on the causes and consequences of international migration on individuals, groups and society (Fong & Li, 2017; Horvath & Amelina, 2017; Startup, 1971). Integration has always been a major subtopic within this field (Castles et al., 2002; Esser, 2006; Heitmeyer & Imbusch, 2005). Early sociological studies focused on the assimilation process of migrants in mainstream society. Due to the harsh criticism of ethnocentrism and ideological bias (Schneider & Crul, 2010), the European scientific community has widely rejected the theories and concepts of assimilation for decades (Alba & Nee, 1997) and prefers the concept of 'integration'. Despite being generally considered less problematic, the term 'integration' has also been subject to heated debates (Schinkel, 2018) and is—at least at the political level—deeply

DOI: 10.4324/9781003370673-2

connected to hegemonic and nationalist endeavours. According to Esser (2006), integration is broadly defined as the inclusion of actors in an existing social system[1] and occurs in four dimensions: cultural, structural, social, and emotional.[2] From a processual perspective, integration is likely to be long term, inter-generational, and subject to drawbacks (Castles et al., 2014; Oberg, 2006). Recent literature differentiates between various outcomes of integration and describes this process as including changes in mainstream society (Schneider & Crul, 2010). Refugee studies (Malkki, 1995) and the sociology of forced migration are particularly relevant in this research (Stepputat & Sørensen, 2014). Building on other academic and non-academic fields, refugee studies emerged as an interdisciplinary discursive domain in the 1970s (Malkki, 1995, p. 507). This particular research area focuses on the causes and consequences of forced migration (Black, 2001), has produced a multitude of case studies but has also struggled to develop a comprehensive synopsis and an adequate theoretical framework (Malkki, 1995, p. 507).

The sociology of sport investigates the reciprocal influences between sport and society (Bette, 2010). It examines 'the role, function and meaning of sport in the lives of people and the societies they form' (Malcolm, 2012, p. 15). As in the case of its mother discipline sociology, sport sociology has undergone a process of differentiation since its emergence in the mid-1960s. Today, the topics subsumed under this area of research include many phenomena on different performance levels, disciplines, roles, and settings (Craig, 2016). Despite these developments, the sociology of sport faces challenges from the natural sciences, from mainstream sociology and from an internal lack of intellectual innovation (Bairner, 2012, p. 103). The aim of this research is to analyse several facets of a complex phenomenon in the context of sport and to understand their relationships. The facets touched upon include classic themes of the sociology of sport at the macro (politics, media, economy), meso (sport organisations, reception centres, refugee sites), and micro (biographies, discrimination, conflict) levels (Coakley & Dunning, 2000; Craig, 2016; Giulianotti, 2015; Malcolm, 2012; Thiel et al., 2013). The relevant information on these themes will be unravelled under an overarching framework in the theory chapter and when assessing and discussing the results.

The combination of these two distinct sociologies is anticipated to effectively support the exploration of the role of sport during the 'refugee crisis'. To date, the topic *migration and sport* is considered to be a distinct and established research area explored by the sociologies of both migration and of sport. The sociological community focuses on two sub-topics in depth, which are of relevance for the present book: labour market immigration and integration in/through sport, which will be briefly summarised hereafter.

Sport as a global phenomenon has a unique relationship with contemporary migration (Giulianotti & Robertson, 2004). The most popular disciplines create a circulation of professional players, typically from the peripheries and semi-peripheries of the world system of sport to the top leagues (Carter, 2011; Darby, 2013; Darby et al., 2007; Lanfranchi & Taylor, 2001). This movement as a form of 'capacity drain' is embedded in the dynamics of power, which impoverishes the countries of origin and enriches those of destination (McGovern, 2002; C.-G. Scott, 2015). Building on Maguire's pioneering work, various studies identify typologies or rather ideal types of migrant athletes (Agergaard, 2008; Magee & Sugden, 2002; Maguire, 1996, 2004b). Politics traditionally presents the inclusion of players with a foreign background in national teams as a demonstration of the emergence of a multicultural society (Seiberth et al., 2017). However, sport has often been a fertile ground for the expression of ethnic, regional, and racial animosities (Back et al., 1999).

The political discourse depicts sport as a powerful integration tool (Council of Europe, 2020; European Commission, 2007; German Federal Government, 2007). While scientific results partly corroborate the integrative effect of sport, its role in this context can neither be taken for granted nor accepted unconditionally (Smith et al., 2019). As stated above, the idea of integration even when related to sport may conceal and support hegemonic discourses (Agergaard, 2018). On the one hand, sport is widely considered a bonding activity that stimulates (intercultural-) contact, is open, egalitarian and due to its body-centredness speaks 'no language'. On the other hand, sociological research has disclosed phenomena of exclusion, cultural closure, and discrimination in sport (Thiel & Seiberth, 2020). For example, sports clubs are one of the most widespread formal organisations in civil society, are characterised by low entry barriers and have a history of inclusive practice towards migrants (S. Braun & Nobis, 2011; Nagel et al., 2020). However, the underrepresentation of segments of the migrant population, as well as processes of exclusion, discrimination, and othering within sports clubs have been widely discussed in the sociology of sport (Dowling, 2020; Seiberth & Thiel, 2010; Seiberth et al., 2013).

Existing literature analyses of migration and sport provide a good overview of the topic at hand from a sociological perspective (Caperchione et al., 2009; Caperchione et al., 2011; Elling et al., 2001;

O'Driscoll et al., 2014; Smith et al., 2019). Many lessons we can glean from these studies on migrants are transferable and adaptable to refugees. These studies have, for example, generated the following relevant knowledge:

- Migration is a process that may imply different experiences and triggers specific coping mechanisms that are related to sport in certain cases.
- Migrants are a highly heterogeneous group that escapes generalisations, in general and with regard to sport preferences, in particular.
- Although sport is often described as such, it is not *per se* an instrument of social integration.
- Migrants are underrepresented in sport, except for male youths, and in some sport disciplines only.
- Sport labour migration is a rising phenomenon in globalised professional sport.

The production of up-to-date knowledge on refugees in sport as a specific target group at this particular historical moment is relevant and crucial (Middleton et al., 2020). In fact, the differences between migrants and refugees are not limited to their type of migration, which is per definition involuntary (Castles, 2003). Despite being a heterogeneous group, refugees share a common legal status and a common background of forced migration (Malkki, 1995). While no typical refugee experience exists (Malkki, 1996), a refugee background often involves adverse life events (but not necessarily traumas) such as passive or active involvement in war events, loss of or separation from family members, a dangerous journey to the country of asylum, prolonged periods in refugee sites and uncertain prospects of permanent residence (Binder & Tošić, 2005; Ha & Lyras, 2013; Hartley et al., 2017). For these reasons, knowledge developed on other migrant groups is only in part transferable to refugees.

2.2 Knowledge on forced migration and sport

Three systematic literature analyses on the topic forced migration and sport have recently been published (Michelini, 2020b; Middleton et al., 2020; Spaaij et al., 2019). These three reviews represent the foundation to illustrate the state of research in this field, to uncover gaps and to demonstrate how this book will build on existing research and fill in some of the gaps.

State of the Art Research 11

A recent literature review (Spaaij et al., 2019) provides an integrative, critical review of scientific literature on forced migration and sport. It synthesises what is known about the experiences of people with a forced migration background with sport and physical activity, and identifies key issues and directions for future projects in this field. The literature review comprises 83 publications published between 1996 and 2019. It reveals a substantial increase in the volume of published research articles on the topic in recent years, and that these publications are primarily concentrated in Western countries around the themes of health promotion, integration, and social inclusion, as well as the obstacles to and facilitators for participation in sport and physical activity. The review also reveals that there is a lack of biographical research on the topic forced migration and sport. Based on this synthesis, four gaps and limitations that require attention in future research have been identified: (1) the experiential (embodied emotional) dimensions of sport and physical activity; (2) the need to decolonise research; (3) space for innovative methodologies, and (4) research ethics.

Middleton et al. (2020) conducted a meta-synthesis of qualitative research studies on forced migrants. By applying a sport psychological lens, the study synthesises multi-disciplinary research from a sample of 23 peer-reviewed journal articles published since 1990, including many sociological studies. Similar to the other two literature reviews considered here, the authors identify the leading themes as the psychosocial benefits of sport, sport as an integrative agent, and barriers to sport. The article highlights how forced migrants' life stories can deliver an understanding of their sport experiences, (also) in comparison with those of voluntary migrants, and emphasises the relevance of feelings of safety in their lives and in sport. The authors also stress the need for a critical approach to better understand how host communities can develop safe and integrative sport and physical activity contexts for forced migrants.

Finally, the author of this book carried out a literature review (Michelini, 2020b) and identified 26 suitable articles published after 2010. In accordance with their discipline, content, and objective, the articles were classified into a health sciences and a sociology group, which were evaluated separately. The articles in the health sciences group address the barriers to participation in physical activity, the evaluation of health-promoting interventions, and the impact of physical activity and sport on health. While assuming that physical activity has a beneficial influence on health, some articles recommend professionals with a broad range of expertise to design and implement

12 State of the Art Research

interventions for refugees based on sport and physical activity. The articles in the sociology group deal with the psychosocial effects of sport, the obstacles to participation in sport as well as the impact of forced migration on sport careers. The literature review confirms the general assumption that sport can have certain positive effects for refugees, e.g. by integrating them, thereby creating a feeling of belonging, and by supporting the process of acculturation (Berry, 2015). These positive effects cannot, however, be generalised due to the high heterogeneity of refugees and the non-representative survey sample. Moreover, the negative effects of participation in sport, such as violence, discrimination and the exploitation of refugee athletes diminish this optimistic outlook. The full article on the literature review is contained in the annexes (articles by the author: 8).

2.3 Critical review of the literature

The weakness of the literature reviews considered above is that they ignore important research studies on forced migration and sport by authors, who for disparate reasons do not use the terms 'refugee' or 'forced migrant' in their publications, despite partially including them in their samples. The extensive work of Sine Agergaard (Agergaard, 2008, 2018, 2019; Agergaard & Engh, 2017; Agergaard, Michelsen la Cour, & Gregersen, 2016; Agergaard & Ryba, 2014), in particular, must be mentioned in this regard. Moreover, by focussing on scientific literature published in English only, the above literature analyses ignore the works of important authors outside the Anglosphere. In the literature on forced migration and sport published in German, which is of particular relevance for this book, the leading authors include Ulrike Burrmann (Burrmann, 2017, 2020; Burrmann, Brandmann, & Chudaske, 2015; Burrmann, Mutz, & Zender, 2015) Sebastian Braun (Braun, 2011, 2018; Braun & Finke, 2010; Braun & Nobis, 2011; Burrmann et al., 2014), Klaus Seiberth (Seiberth, 2010, 2012; Seiberth & Thiel, 2014; Seiberth, Thiel, & Hanke, 2018; Seiberth, Weigelt-Schlesinger, & Schlesinger, 2013; Thiel & Seiberth, 2020) and Tina Nobis (Albert & Nobis, 2020; Nobis, 2013, 2017; Nobis & Bauer, 2007).[3]

More generally, the articles identified and examined in the systematic literature reviews are insufficient to accurately represent the many social phenomena that emerged in the field of sport during the 'refugee crisis'. With the exception of research on sports clubs (Feuchter & Janetzko, 2018; Michelini et al., 2018; Nowy, Feiler, & Breuer, 2020; Seiberth et al., 2018; Straume et al., 2018; Tuchel et al., 2021; Verweyen, 2019), most of the articles ignore the topics this book delves into, namely the

State of the Art Research 13

mass media discourse on sport in the context of the 'refugee crisis', the role of sport in refugee sites, and the careers of elite athletes with a refugee background. The current status of research on *migration and sport* is in part transferrable to the sub-field this book explores and represents a solid foundation for performing further scientific studies tailored to refugees. Yet due to its specificity and social relevance, refugee-focused research deserves innovative, more inclusive and ambitious studies. Small-scale and cross-sectional studies have produced some empirical-based knowledge on this topic. Sports sociologists, as well as many social scientists, are still conducting research and publishing results on this topic, based primarily on small, local, and explorative projects. This book aims to create bridges between the four projects the author was involved in and other research programmes. The systematic literature review presented in this chapter (Michelini, 2020b) is a collection, synthesis and critical evaluation of research studies on forced migration and sport. Two articles contained in this book (Michelini et al., 2018; Tuchel et al., 2021) resulted from the merging of data from the project *Activities for Refugees in Sports Clubs* with those of two similar projects[4] carried out in Germany by other research teams. Finally, this book itself is an effort to connect the author's different research projects with one another. While each individual project presented in the following chapters adds yet another small and fragmented piece of knowledge to the current state of research, their consideration within an overall study provides a more general and broader overview of the topic *forced migration and sport*.

Notes

1 At a more abstract level, integration indicates the cohesion of different parts (function systems, organisations, groups, and individuals) of a system (Esser, 2006, p. 7).
2 The number, label, and contents of these dimensions differ in other theories of integration (Ager & Strang, 2008).
3 The quotations in this paragraph entail also sources, which were written by more authors or co-authored by the mentioned researchers.
4 The project *Sport for and with Refugees* was carried out at the Technical University of Chemnitz, and the project *Refugee Work of Sport Clubs* was conducted at the Humboldt University Berlin.

3 Definitions of Key Terms in Forced Migration and Sport

This chapter defines the key terms used in this book. Concepts related to migration, physical activity, and crises lie at the core of the topic analysed here. To give the reader a better understanding of the present discussion, these concepts must be introduced, explained, and delimited from and related to each other. Indeed, many of these words are politically charged and used with dissimilar meanings in different social contexts. The theoretical implications of the definitions, which are borrowed from existing glossaries and scientific literature, will be discussed in detail and further deepened in successive chapters.

3.1 Migrant, displaced person, and refugee

These terms have been chosen, amongst many others, from the vast lexicon on migration because of their particular relevance for this research.[1] Taking a juridical perspective has the advantage of providing precise yet neutral definitions of these terms, with relevant and concrete implications. Other related concepts can be found in the *Glossary on Migration* based on international migration law (Sironi et al., 2019). According to this source:

> Migration involves '[t]he movement of persons away from their place of usual residence, either across an international border or within a State' (Sironi et al., 2019, p. 137). In turn, a migrant is a person, 'who moves away from his or her place of usual residence, whether within a country or across an international border, temporarily or permanently, and for a variety of reasons' (Sironi et al., 2019, p. 132). Importantly, migrant is understood here in an inclusivist and not in a residualist sense (Sironi et al., 2019, p. 133). Therefore, as an umbrella term, it also includes those who have fled war or persecution.

DOI: 10.4324/9781003370673-3

Definitions of Key Terms 15

Forced migration is used here as a synonym for displacement and is defined as 'a migratory movement which, although the drivers can be diverse, involves force, compulsion, or coercion' (Sironi et al., 2019, p. 77). Displaced persons 'have been forced or obliged to flee or to leave their homes or places of habitual residence, [...] in particular as a result of or in order to avoid the effects of armed conflict, situations of generalized violence, violations of human rights or natural or human-made disasters' (Sironi et al., 2019, p. 77).

The 1951 United Nations Convention on the Status of Refugees and its 1967 Protocol defines a refugee as:

> *[a] person who, owing to a well-founded fear of persecution for reasons of race, religion, nationality, membership of a particular social group or political opinion, is outside the country of his nationality and is unable or, owing to such fear, is unwilling to avail himself of the protection of that country; or who, not having a nationality and being outside the country of his former habitual residence as a result of such events, is unable or, owing to such fear, is unwilling to return to it.*
>
> (UNHCR, 2010, p. 14)

Refugees are recognised as such through a formal determination procedure (C. Hardy, 2003) based on objective criteria related to the circumstances of their displacement, 'which justify a presumption that they meet the criteria of the applicable refugee definition' (Sironi et al., 2019, p. 14). An asylum seeker, on the other hand, is an individual, 'who is seeking international protection. In countries with individualized procedures, an asylum seeker is someone, whose claim has not been finally decided yet by the country in which he or she has submitted it. Not every asylum seeker will in the end be recognized as a refugee, but every recognized refugee is initially an asylum seeker' (Sironi et al., 2019, p. 14). Figure 3.1 shows a possible typology of migrants and the position of refugees in it.

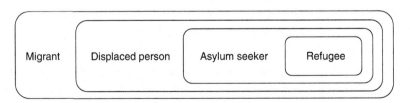

Figure 3.1 A typology of migrants.

16 Definitions of Key Terms

Importantly, while according to the Universal Declaration of Human Rights '[e]veryone has the right to seek and to enjoy in other countries asylum from persecution' (UN, 1948, Article 14.1), being a recognised refugee rests on claiming and being granted such status. For a variety of reasons, not every displaced person with the possibility of being granted refugee status actually claims it. Moreover, not every person who meets the criteria and claims this status is recognised as being a refugee. In fact, a formal determination of refugee status is subject to variables such as the work of case reviewers and socio-political factors. European migration policy has been extensively criticised for (amongst other reasons) creating a dichotomy between (encouraged) economic migration and (discouraged) asylum migration (Stewart, 2008). During the 'refugee crisis', for example, several European countries accelerated or prioritised asylum procedures for refugees from selected countries, notably from Syria (Asylum Information Database, 2017). The asylum-migration nexus—or rather the acknowledgement of an overlapping relationship between irregular and asylum migration—is widely accepted in the sociology of migration (Stewart, 2008, p. 224). For this reason, this research does not limit its focus on refugees and also includes displaced persons in general.

The definitions introduced above are products of the modern political order. There is a dynamic legal and political discussion on the typology of refugees and on the admission of new types, notably that of internally displaced persons, environmental refugees and development-induced refugees (Black, 2001). Social science has traditionally taken a critical attitude towards the social construction of these labels and towards the process of their social acceptance (Black, 2001, p. 63). Moreover, the term 'refugee' becomes misleading when used to label generalisable types of persons, identities, cultures, communities, or situations without specific historicisation and contextualisation (Malkki, 1995, p. 496). This book therefore avoids using generalising concepts such as the 'refugee experience' (Agier, 2008) or the 'refugee psychological condition' (Thompson et al., 2018) without considering the broader social, political, and personal context.

3.2 Physical activity, exercise, and sport

Drawing from widely accepted definitions in sport sciences, physical activity (PA) is defined as 'any bodily movement produced by skeletal muscles that results in energy expenditure above resting level' (Bouchard & Shephard, 1994, p. 77). This definition embraces all possible human activities involving movement in leisure, work,

Definitions of Key Terms 17

commuting, and household domains (Cavill et al., 2006, p. 3). PA can further be characterised by considering its mode, intensity, duration, frequency, and continuity (Ainsworth et al., 2000). (Caspersen et al. (1985, p. 126)) define *exercise* as 'a subset of physical activity that is planned, structured, and repetitive and has as a final or an intermediate objective the improvement or maintenance of physical fitness'. Exercise is leisure PA carried out with the purpose of improving or maintaining one or more physical fitness components (Caspersen et al., 1985, p. 128; Pietilä et al., 1995, p. 330).

As an activity and a social construct (Heinemann, 2007), sport and its connection to the 'refugee crisis' lie at the core of this research. Sport shares many characteristics with what Brunner et al., (1972–1997) call 'basic concepts' (*Grundbegriffe*), which are inevitable and irreplaceable in the political and social vocabulary. Historically, the meaning of sport changed widely before crystallising into its modern meaning.[2] Nevertheless, and despite being a global term, its interpretation still depends on geographic, linguistic, and cultural factors (Loy, 1968; Thiel et al., 2013). This may be the reasons why philosophers and sociologists continue to be engaged in discussions about the definition of sport (Klein, 2016). While this book considers sport primarily as a social construct (Heinemann, 1998, p. 53), this section defines sport as a type of PA with unique characteristics. The German sociologist Heinemann (2007, p. 56) identifies four characteristics that are fundamental to sport: (1) it is a PA that involves the human body; (2) it is performance-oriented; (3) it is 'autotelic', i.e. it has a purpose in itself; (4) it is governed by specific rules.

Interestingly, despite the fact that the terms 'PA', 'exercise', and 'sport' are precise, definable, and distinguishable, they have become increasingly conflated and used synonymously (Haag et al., 2012, p. 264; Waddington et al., 1997, p. 170). Particularly, the word 'sport' itself has been de-sportified (Bette, 1995; Cachay, 1990; Digel, 1990; Grupe, 1988), and is often used for PAs that do not exhibit the fundamental characteristics of sport. An upcoming section of this chapter argues that aside from being a type of PA, sport is also a social construct (Heinemann, 2007) or rather, according to this theoretical framework, a function system (Bette, 1989; Schimank, 1988).

3.3 Crisis and migration crises

'Crisis' is a basic and over-inflated concept in the political and social vocabulary (Koselleck & Richter, 2006). Its modern meaning 'refers to a sudden change, a temporal interruption of a condition of normality'

18 Definitions of Key Terms

(Carastathis et al., 2018). Abundant sociological research deals with specific crises, especially economic ones. While Marxism (Engels, 1844/1996; Marx, 1867/2018), systems theory (Luhmann, 1987b; Parsons, 1951) and critical theory (Habermas, 1980) deliver in-depth theorisations of crisis as a social phenomenon, the term remains elusive. It has ancient Greek origins (from κρίσις 'decision') and its usage has been transforming and plurivalent from early on (Holton, 1987; Koselleck & Richter, 2006; O'Conner, 1981). From a historical perspective, Koselleck and Richter (2006, p. 358) observe that:

> *since 1780, [crisis] has become an expression of a new sense of time which both indicated and intensified the end of an epoch. Perceptions of such epochal change can be measured by the increased use of crisis. But the concept remains as multi-layered and ambiguous as the emotions attached to it. Conceptualized as chronic, 'crisis' can also indicate a state of greater or lesser permanence, as in a longer or shorter transition towards something better or worse or towards something altogether different. 'Crisis' can announce a recurring event, as in economics, or become an existential term of analysis, as in psychology and theology.*

They conclude their analysis of the concept of crisis with an admonition to scholars to weigh the implication of this concept carefully before adopting it for analytical aims (Koselleck & Richter, 2006, p. 400). This book examines a crisis that was indubitably perceived as such, and the author does not use the term 'crisis' as a catch-term.

The frequent usage of the term 'crisis' could indicate 'semantic-bleaching' (Meillet, 1912/1965) or a contemporary tendency of society to describe itself as being permanently inflicted by crises (Holton, 1987; Luhmann, 1984a). Alternatively, this may reflect a concrete rise in crises in our 'high-speed society' (Rosa, 2003) or may reinforce the suggestion of Biggs et al. (2011) that we are indeed entering an era of concatenated global crises. In any case, if we consider crises as a state contrary to normality, we are witnessing a paradoxical normalisation of the crisis-state (Holton, 1987, p. 503).

Concerning the definition of the term crisis, Koselleck and Richter (2006) identify four main understandings of the concept of crisis, namely as:

1 A chain of events that culminate in a situation that requires decisive action.

Definitions of Key Terms 19

2 A turning-point after which human conditions will change forever.
3 A situation that endangers the existence of an entity, system or status quo.
4 A transitional phase made necessary by the inherent logic or prior developments.

The elusive concept of crisis can therefore be understood in different ways. At the core of its varying definitions, however, lies the idea of a radical change with widespread impacts on different areas and levels of society. The concepts of nation-state and citizenship are crucial to the modern social order. Therefore, migrations, particularly when massive, unexpected and cross-national, have a considerable disrupting power (Maehler & Brinkmann, 2015, p. 164). As previous migration crises have, the so-called 'refugee crisis' widely impacted society, as the next chapter will argue.

Notes

1 Further definitions such as 'stateless person' and 'humanitarian refugee' are not included.
2 The etymology of the word 'sport', a short form of the old French *desport*, signifies amusement and play (Haag et al., 2012, p. 472).

4 The 'Refugee Crisis'

The 'refugee crisis' represents the central phenomenon of this book. Its heated political and media discussion—particularly between 2015 and 2016—acknowledges it as being widely influential under economic, political, and social aspects. However, it must be stressed that refugee-receiving nations in West Asia and North Africa received much larger numbers of refugees in the years prior to 2015–2016 than Europe without earning the same kind of attention or framing it in similar public and political narratives. The social construction of the 'refugee crisis' in Europe erases the long-term processes underlying it from consideration and reinforces the Eurocentric assumption that these long-term processes 'exploded' when Europe became affected (Fiddian-Qasmiyeh, 2016). Therefore, the opinion of many activists and sociologists is that the phenomenon has been widely constructed as a crisis and that it has been instrumentalised as such. Explaining its impact on society and in particular on the sport system requires a description of the 'crisis' both as a social context and as a process. This chapter thereby aims to furnish a sufficient contextual backdrop for the reader to better understand the ensuing arguments of this book and to understand the reasons beyond its polarised discussion.

4.1 The context of the 'refugee crisis'

While a comprehensive analysis of the 'refugee crisis' exceeds the ambitions of this chapter, its brief description as a social phenomenon and its position in the present discussion is important for understanding this research.

The 'refugee crisis' was an episode within a historical pattern of migration to Europe (Bade, 2008), which was closely connected with the civil war in Syria.[1] According to media reports (Aljazeera, 2018; BBC, 2019; CNN, 2020), this ongoing multi-sided civil war began in 2011.

DOI: 10.4324/9781003370673-4

It has developed into one of the bloodiest and most complex conflicts in the world today, since it involves dynamic and numerous coalitions of adversaries opposing each other in varying combinations. Amongst other consequences for the neighbouring countries, this conflict caused a migration movement of populations to Europe, where asylum applications have surged since 2013 (Eurostat, 2020). This, as well as a concatenation of further events, which are partly illustrated in the figure below,[2] evolved in Europe as a complex social phenomenon that was referred to and constructed as the 'refugee crisis' (Figure 4.1).

Here, the 'refugee crisis' is considered to be a type of migration crisis or rather 'the complex and often large-scale migration flows and mobility patterns caused by a crisis, which typically involve significant vulnerabilities for individuals and affected communities and generate acute and longer-term migration management challenges' (Sironi et al., 2019, p. 137). The massive arrival of refugees in Europe during this period affected all countries and unleashed a chain of consequences in different social domains. This, in turn, created a situation that was perceived in Europe as being alarming:

> *Europe is in the midst of an unprecedented human migration. Fleeing war, fearing for their life and dreaming of a better life far from the poverty and upheaval of their unstable nations, hundreds of thousands are flocking to Europe's shores. The migrants and refugees risk their lives in rickety boats and cramped lorry containers – only to be greeted by governments that can't agree on how, or if, to welcome them.*
> (Smith-Spark, 2015)

In this sense, despite the misleading political usage of this term, it is appropriate to speak of a 'refugee crisis'. Nevertheless, this book uses scare quotes when referring to the 'refugee crisis' to depict the author's critical attitude towards the negative, problematised and politicised understanding of this expression, which was constructed at the ideological level through the convergence of media, affect, and politics (Gutiérrez Rodríguez, 2018, p. 17).

Numerous sociologists (Brändle et al., 2019; Carastathis et al., 2018; Fotopoulos & Kaimaklioti, 2016; Gutiérrez Rodríguez, 2018; Holmes & Castañeda, 2016; Krzyżanowski et al., 2018; Lams, 2018; Moore et al., 2018; Rheindorf & Wodak, 2018; Sigona, 2018; Weber, 2016) have discussed and criticised the racist, nationalist, and colonialist features of the political and media construction of the 'refugee crisis'. Georgiou and Zaborowski (2017, p. 3) note that the narratives of the coverage on

22 The 'Refugee Crisis'

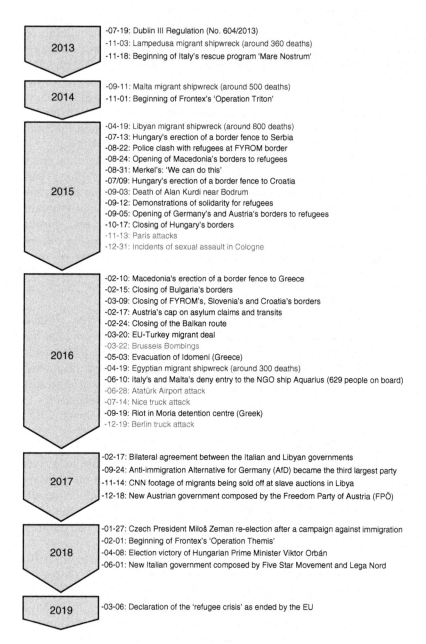

Figure 4.1 Timeline of the European 'refugee crisis'.

refugees changed over time: 'The sympathetic and empathetic response of a large proportion of the European press in the summer and especially early autumn of 2015 was gradually replaced by suspicion and, in some cases, hostility towards refugees and migrants'. Interestingly, even the mainstream nomenclature of this phenomenon changed from the *summer of migration* to the '*refugee crisis*' (Gutiérrez Rodríguez, 2018, p. 17). This reflects a broader development of the attitude towards refugees, who initially sparked intense feelings of solidarity that appealed to Christian and humanitarian traditions of charity and empathy, or rather to the so-called *Willkommenskultur* embodied by the motto 'Refugees Welcome'. After a series of terrorist attacks and other events, such as sexual assaults on women on New Year's Eve 2015/2016 in Cologne,[3] this compassionate attitude was gradually replaced by a more distrustful one, which in the opinion of some critical sociologists occasionally crossed over into racial constructions of refugees as the 'Other' and was submerged in colonial imaginary (Gutiérrez Rodríguez, 2018).

In the public perception (Zick et al., 2008) and in media portrayals (Georgiou & Zaborowski, 2017), refugees were often represented as outsiders and as being different to Europeans through ascribed connotations that were either positive (vulnerable outsiders) or negative (dangerous outsiders). Either way, refugees were constructed as the 'Other' from a European perspective (Dussel, 1995). The political discourse described the integration of refugees as an evidently challenging task:

> *Thus within the media rhetoric of the "refugee crisis," the signifier of the "refugee" works as a "floating signifier" representing the anxieties and fears of what the media conceived as the majority of the population, regularly imagined as white, German, abled, cisgendered, national bodies. These anxieties and fears of the presumed population are projected onto an imagined racialized Other. Further, the link of the "refugee" with "crisis" points to the idea of rupture and singularity. As Myrto Tsilimpounidi notes, "crisis" can be perceived as a "perpetual frame-breaking moment that dismantles the certainties and normative narratives of nation, sovereignty, social bonds and belonging for people on the ground." "Crisis" involves financial, economic, or political life in dominant media and political discourses, but also defines a "state of being" in society that results out of a "deep political and social sense of uncertainty, precarity, and dispossession." Linked to refugees, the media and political rhetoric on "crisis" illustrates the continuation of the coloniality of power.*
>
> (Gutiérrez Rodríguez, 2018, p. 19)

4.2 The 'refugee crisis' as a process

The 'refugee crisis' is a process that can be broken down into a distinct number of consecutive time frames. As will be argued in a forthcoming chapter on Germany, this phenomenon from a European perspective can be divided into three phases based on asylum applications (Figure 4.2): pre-peak (2013–2014), peak (2015–2016), and post-peak (2017–2018).

The pre-peak phase of the 'refugee crisis' is deeply connected to events that took place far away from Europe, and included wars, human rights violations, environmental and climate catastrophes, and economic hardship. Among these events, the Syrian Civil War played a key role. This ongoing multi-sided armed conflict began in 2011 as a series of protests that President Bashar al-Assad's government repressed violently (Aljazeera, 2016; BBC, 2016c; CNN, 2016). A crackdown by the Syrian Army, the formation of several fighting factions and the increasing interference of foreign nations followed. Consequently, a gradually increasing number of displaced persons began leaving Syria to seek safe harbour in neighbouring countries or in Europe, and were joined by other migrant groups. The number of asylum applications in the EU reached 400,515 in 2013, and 594,180 in 2014 (Eurostat, 2020). Prior to the peak phase, the phenomenon was mostly a media topic and the socio-political attitude towards the arriving refugees was generally positive (Georgiou & Zaborowski, 2017). The Syrian Civil War was widely reported in European mass media and the conflict was increasingly perceived as a distant yet relevant event.

The European 'refugee crisis' reached its peak between 2015 and 2016. Together with people migrating to Europe for other reasons,

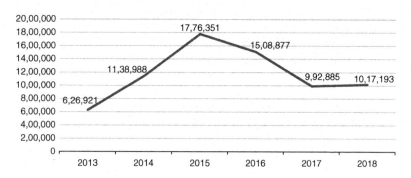

Figure 4.2 Asylum applications in Europe between 2013 and 2018 (UNHCR, 2022a).

over five million Syrians sought safety first in neighbouring countries and later in Europe. During this phase, which includes what has been called the 'long summer of migration', a massive stream of Syrian, Afghan, and Iraqi forced migrants reached Europe, mostly through Italy or Greece and the 'Balkan route' (UNHCR, 2021). According to data of Eurostat (2020), asylum applications more than doubled in comparison to previous years and exceeded the 1 million mark in both 2015 (1,282,690) and 2016 (1,221,185). There is broad consensus that the pervasive mass media's reporting was fundamental in co-creating the crisis and that it made it tangible, even where its consequences were not palpable (Krzyżanowski et al., 2018). The mediatisation of single national and international events such as the tragic death of toddler Alan Kurdi (Vollmer & Karakayali, 2018) or the sexual assaults on women on New Year's Eve 2015/2016 in Cologne (Weber, 2016) played an important role in mobilising public opinion in support of or against refugees (Georgiou & Zaborowski, 2017). During this phase of the 'refugee crisis', this social phenomenon intensified and represented a notable irritation for society as a whole.

After the peak of the crisis had been reached, political measures were taken to limit the migration streams to Europe (Krzyżanowski et al., 2018). Importantly, the EU-Turkey Deal (2016) and the bilateral agreement between the Governments of Italy and Libya (2017) contributed to a drastic reduction in the number of migrants entering European countries (Becatoros, 2019). These deals were met with criticism due to their (lack of humanitarian) goals and the entrustment of countries with a questionable resolve or capacity to respect international law and ensure appropriate protection of refugees (Amnesty International, 2016; Engin, 2017; Gkliati, 2017; Hakura, 2016). The number of asylum applications in the EU dropped to 677,470 in 2017 and to 608,335 in 2018 (Eurostat, 2020). This notwithstanding, the socio-political discussion remained negative and critical towards the welcome culture. It focused mainly on problems connected to the 'refugee crisis', amongst others, migrant criminality, repatriation and (failed) integration. To put an end to the distorted use of this topic for political campaigns, the EU declared the 'refugee crisis' as being over in March 2019 (Rankin, 2019). Apart from some temporary abatement, the media's attention on the 'refugee crisis' remained very high in the years following the peak phase. Only the new crisis triggered by the COVID-19 pandemic has been able to turn the spotlight away from the 'refugee crisis' and to monopolise the media's attention (Bortoletto et al., 2021). In turn, this was fundamental to end the intensive discussion on migration to the EU and therefore the 'refugee crisis'.

4.3 Sport in the 'refugee crisis'

As previously stated, the 'refugee crisis' affected European society to different degrees and at various levels. Intuitively, the widespread and radical changes caused by the 'refugee crisis' may have also impacted sport in four fundamental ways. First, as an external impulse, it may have indirectly fostered adaptation processes originating within the sport system. For example, a sport federation might admit refugees without a club affiliation to a competition to adapt to the special social situation (*Zeitgeist*). Second, the 'refugee crisis' may have had an indirect impact on sport through other areas of society. This is the case when politics call for (non-bindingly or bindingly) cooperation of sport in managing the crisis. Third, sport may have developed internal adaptation processes. This is the case when sports clubs' human resources decide to organise sport offers for refugees. Finally, fourth, the inclusion of refugees in sport may have induced change. For example, the presence of refugees in sports clubs may have influenced the clubs' programmes. While the first two effects represent quasi top-down and the last two quasi bottom-up processes, how social adaptation evolves is always complex, overlapping, and embedded in multiple processes and requires the support of a refined theoretical framework. The concepts introduced in the next chapter will allow for a more sophisticated consideration of the role of sport in the 'refugee crisis'.

Notes

1 In 2015, among the over one million refugees that arrived in Europe, 46.7 per cent were Syrian, 20.9 per cent were Afghan, and 9.4 per cent were Iraqi (UNHCR, 2021).
2 The figure was created by the author based on different sources (amongst others: Carlson et al., 2018; Dockery, 2017; Fry, 2015; Rheindorf & Wodak, 2018; Weesjes, 2016).
3 Importantly, the alleged involvement of refugees as the perpetrators of these events was later disclaimed (BBC, 2016b), and the political use of these circumstances was heavily criticised (Weber, 2016).

5 Systems Theoretical Framework

To elucidate the poly-contextural embeddedness of the observed phenomenon (Günther, 1979), this book applies an overarching theoretical framework based on Luhmann's systems theory (1987b) to re-analyse and re-interpret the data collected for four research projects on the topic forced migration and sport. This enables a comparison and contrasting of the individual projects and is therefore a premise for creating new knowledge from this process. Part of the projects initially relied on other theoretical frameworks (Table 5.1), including Hurrelmann's interactional concept of socialisation theory (1988) and Foucault's poststructuralist theory (1977).

Table 5.1 Sociological theories applied in the research

Projects	Theory
Sport and Forced Migration in the Mass Media	Foucault's post-structuralist theory
Activities for Refugees in Sports Clubs	Luhmann's systems theory
Physical Activity in Refugee Reception Sites	Luhmann's systems theory
Forced Migration and Elite Sport	Hurrelmann's socialisation theory

This chapter introduces sociological systems theory in detail as the leading framework and subsequently outlines the fundamental components of theories that assumed a secondary role in the research process. Importantly, as systems theory is a general theory, it can absorb further comprehensive sociological theories as well as other specific theories that are better capable of shedding light on selected contexts and facets of this social phenomenon.

DOI: 10.4324/9781003370673-5

5.1 Systems theory

Luhmann's systems theory differs in its fundamental assumptions from other system-based alternatives[1] (Thiel & Tangen, 2015). It was chosen for its ambition to be a super-theory for the description of society (Luhmann, 1984b, p. 19). This sociological theory can be described as a network of ideas, representations and definitions, which relies on shared theoretical foundations. Luhmann's ultimate goal (1982a, p. XIII) was 'to develop a conceptual vocabulary that is refined, variegated, and supple enough to capture what he sees as the unprecedented structural characteristics of modern society'. Its complexity and depth makes it possible in the present case to relate the individual projects to one another under an overarching frame (Willke, 2006, pp. 1–4).

This section introduces general and specific systems theoretical concepts applied to this book's topic and the typification of the systems underlying its research projects. The discussion chapter uses these elements in a more ambitious and applied way by delivering an overarching systems theoretical consideration of the topic *forced migration and sport*. While this book explains—at least briefly—the main systems theoretical concepts that lie at its core, existing secondary and introduction literature on systems theory in the form of glossaries (Baraldi et al., 1997; Krause, 2005; Moeller, 2006) is useful to deepen its theoretical implications and to grasp its inner complexity and requisite variety (Ashby, 1991).

5.1.1 General assumptions

As Luhmann's systems theory is highly abstract and not necessarily intuitive for non-expert readers, the pillars of this theory need to be introduced. Accordingly, 'systems are based on a difference between system and environment. Therefore, system differentiation means the repetition of this difference within systems' (Luhmann, 1984a, p. 63). Amongst other types of systems, 'social systems are self-referential systems based on meaningful communication' (Luhmann, 1982b, p. 131). Communication is the constitutive element of society, i.e. a type of social system that includes all other systems as well as all communications. Different from other social systems, however, society as a self-substitutive order cannot communicate outside itself and actualises its contents through internal circulation. In modernity, society is one complex and unified world system (Luhmann, 1982b).

At the same time, modern society is internally differentiated into subsystems, enabling communication between these systems. Differentiation

Systems Theoretical Framework 29

is 'the emergence of a particular subsystem of society by which the characteristics of system formation, especially autopoietic self-reproduction, self-organization, structural determination and, along with all these, operational closure itself are realized' (Luhmann, 2000, p. 23). Examples of function systems are politics, mass media, education, health, economy, law, family, and sport. Such systems are interconnections of communication related to a social area and to a particular societal problem, such as the production of collectively binding decisions (politics), the circulation of information (mass media) or the distribution of goods (economy). Each system is autopoietic, indicating the ability of self-reproduction and self-maintenance (Maturana & Varela, 1987), but is also strictly coupled to the others by contributing to the (re-)production and integration of society (Luhmann, 2008). Importantly, neither society nor function systems can be dominated by any one of these systems, no matter how indispensable and central its position is, as in the case of politics, health, and economy (Luhmann, 1982b, p. 131). Operationally closed systems cannot directly influence each other's operations in the sense of a simplistic cause-effect relationship. Even in case of strict coupling, the autopoiesis of function systems implies a self-referential reproduction of their constitutive elements. The precondition for the differentiation between function systems is the existence of a specific 'code' (Luhmann, 2000, p. 23), which operationalises systemic logics and delineates their boundaries through a rigid semantic form with an 'either/or' binary structure (Luhmann, 1990, p. 173). According to Luhmann (1987b), society is one type of social system as are organisations and interactions. The typology of systems as conceived by Luhmann and represented in a slightly modified version in Figure 5.1 is one of the few figures created by Luhmann himself, and offers a rough systematic outline of his broad and complex theoretical framework. This might be the reason why it is so well-received by systems theorists (Borch, 2011; Seidl & Becker, 2005; Seidl & Schoeneborn, 2010).

The main objective of Luhmann's typology of systems is to explain 'how and where the connectivity of communication lets systemic orders

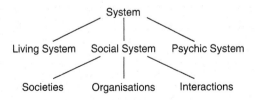

Figure 5.1 A typology of systems.

emerge' (Nassehi, 2005, p. 183). It does not consider levels of generality or aggregation, but instead focuses on types of conditions for the emergence of different types of self-referential systems (Nassehi, 2005, p. 183). Luhmann's typology identifies three types of social systems:

- Societies are encompassing systems that include all possible forms of communication. Modernity is characterised by the emergence of one encompassing world-society and by the differentiation of function systems within society.
- Organisations emerge as communication systems through their capacity to stabilise types of action and behaviour through the decisions organisations take on the basis of specific premises and cultures.
- Interaction is a type of system that implies the co-presence of persons as a delimitation criterion. The ego/alter model of communication determines the subjectivity of face-to-face interactions.

5.1.2 Specific concepts

This section explains the topic of this book—forced migration and sport—through systems theory. Remaining at the abstract level, the following section clarifies how social change is possible and how the 'refugee crisis' fostered adaptation processes in different function systems, particularly in sport.

Without implying progress in a positivist sense, different social phenomena are considered to be a product of the evolution of society (Luhmann et al., 1982). From the perspective of systems theory, society 'is the encompassing social system which includes all communications, reproduces all communications and constitutes meaningful horizons for further communications' (Luhmann, 1982b, p. 131). All forms of communication that emerge from any type of social system are contained within it (Luhmann, 1987b). Society is dynamic because it produces and reproduces itself through elementary operations of social systems, which are oriented towards their respective environments (Luhmann, 1987b, 1997; Stichweh, 2018). New elements, innovations, variations, and crises constitute events that influence this perpetual process of systemic reproduction. The manifestation of an event elicits the difference between 'before' and 'after' and unveils a horizon of references to other possibilities (Baraldi et al., 1997). Events cause instability and a high probability of social change because systems do not only reproduce themselves but also adapt to environmental changes. Society does not plan to evolve or adjust. Instead, this occurs unintentionally through 'useable coincidences' (Luhmann, 1997, p. 417). Adaptations always have a processual character. In Luhmann's work, time is connected to the concept of contingency, especially when the perception of the future is addressed. Time is a premise for the constitution of systems because it allows for the establishment of order through structure and process (Schwanitz, 1995). Both of these forms of order can absorb time and constitute a pattern of expectations that serves as a means of orientation for events. At the most abstract level, this clarifies how social change occurs.

Crises—in this case provoked by a huge mass of displaced persons—are an important environmental novelty that cause social change and have widespread impacts on society. While 'Europe is not the center stage of a global refugee crisis' (Maley, 2016, p. 73), its self-description suggests that it is. Society is a world system, whose boundaries are not set by territorial frontiers (Luhmann, 1982b). The same applies to function systems, which evolved in modernity as lateral world systems (Willke, 2007). The political system still refers to the state as a way of optimising its functions. As this system is responsible for making collectively binding decisions, it reinforces the relevance of the nation-state in tension, but not in contradiction, with strong globalising tendencies (Maguire, 2004a). This book considers Europe as a geographical area[2] that is loosely unified by an historical heritage and a set of social norms, ethical values, traditional customs, belief systems, originated in or associated with it (Perry et al., 2015). Importantly, Europe hosts a political and economic union (EU) of (to date) 27 member states, which emerged from a long and ongoing political process that began after the Second World War (European Union, 2020). While the 'refugee crisis' undeniably affected the entire world, particularly the West Asia region, it developed in the EU as a total social fact (Mauss, 2002), with major implications.

Luhmann's analysis of crises (1984a) does not entail the definition of crisis or its underlying mechanisms of genesis, but instead focuses on its social function. 'Crisis' is a description of a social phenomenon (1) that requires urgent and swift action, (2) spreads across function systems and affects society as a whole, and (3) whose self-description works as a self-fulfilling prophecy (Luhmann, 1984a). All of these elements can be found in the 'refugee crisis', which from a European perspective was a social phenomenon that brought a large mass of displaced persons to Europe, causing a sense of overwhelming pressure. Political actions perceived as being inconsiderate were taken to manage the 'refugee crisis'. One example was the decision to open the German borders to refugees on the 'Balkan route'. The 'crisis' was perceived as influencing different function systems, in particular the economy. The fact that its description as a 'crisis' served as a self-fulfilling prophecy is evident against the backdrop of recent events. With the outbreak of a new crisis, namely the COVID-19 pandemic, the 'refugee crisis' mostly disappeared from mass media reports and political agendas (Bortoletto et al., 2021).

As Agamben (1998) notes, like 'homo sacer', a forced migrant may find him- or herself outside the law or beyond it—a 'bare life', which 'is included in the juridical order solely in the form of its exclusion' (Agamben, 1998, p. 12). The exceptional existence of refugees embodies the contradiction within an established nation-based order. This perhaps is the reason why the 'refugee crisis' and particularly the massive presence of refugees on European soil was largely perceived as a problem of social integration. Society determines the way people are made relevant (and irrelevant) in communication (Schirmer & Michailakis, 2015). Despite the basic universalism of inclusion in modern society, refugees belong to a group of people most at risk of becoming irrelevant to function systems, and thus experience radical forms of exclusion (Luhmann, 1997). The absence of legal documents, in particular, obstructs access to the labour market and to basic care services. The work of international, national and local social work organisations can supervise refugees' re-inclusion in society. Obviously, this does not by any means imply equal access to all function systems.

The differentiation of society and the autopoiesis of systems denote their 'legitimate indifference' (Tyrell, 1978), but also the emergence of chains of reactions throughout all of society when an event reaches the necessary tipping point. As function systems are a type of social system that are highly interconnected to one another and to society, crises have a high likelihood of influencing their reproduction. Their adaptation, however, is always reciprocal, occurs within the self-referentiality, autopoiesis, and operational closure of systems, and is embedded in overlapping and mostly simultaneously co-existing social processes. This also applies to the autopoiesis of all function systems, because they are strictly coupled both with one another and with the environment (Luhmann, 2008). While no system can dominate the other or exert influence without being influenced itself (Moeller, 2006, p. 39), the environment can impact systems in different ways, a concept that in systems theory is referred to as an 'irritation'.[3]

Sport is one of the many function systems that is differentiated in modern society (Bette, 1989; Cachay, 1988; Cachay & Thiel, 2000; Schimank, 1988). It is specialised in the communication of physical performances (Stichweh, 1990, p. 380) through the code 'victory/defeat'

(Schimank, 1988, p. 185). From this viewpoint, sport communications interpret physical movements through a sports-related institutionalised vocabulary and focus (Stichweh, 1990, p. 379), oriented towards competition. Sport descriptions abstract many features and details of sport events by reducing them into measurable and relevant information (Stichweh, 1990, p. 379). This reduction ensures not only the possibility of understanding but also of comparing expected and completed sport performances, which in turn causes the spread of communication (Stichweh, 1990, p. 379). Sport is a multifaceted, complex and differentiated system that relies on privileged structural couplings with other systems, particularly mass media, health, politics, and the economy (Bette & Schimank, 2006, pp. 90–116; Schimank, 2001, pp. 13–15; 2008, p. 72). Amongst other examples, sport is observable in mass media communications (television, newspapers, internet, radio), in the operation of both sport organisations (clubs, federations, leagues) and non-sport organisations (schools, prisons, camps), and in the performance of athletes (elite, amateur, and informal). The results and discussion chapters will explore concrete cases of these specific examples.

Following decades of development, the sport system has evolved into a complex and differentiated structure with several centres and many subsystems tightly or loosely connected with one another (Stichweh, 2013, p. 93). Stichweh (1990, p. 378; also in Thiel & Tangen, 2015, p. 77) characterises sport in modernity as being internally divided into different fields of sport. While Stichweh neither discusses nor describes this differentiation in depth, his intuitive and simple categorisation of fields of sport is ordered according to the decreasing centrality of performance, which this book interprets as follows (Heinemann, 2007; Stichweh, 1990; Willimczik, 2007):

- Elite sport is primarily oriented towards competition and is practised by professional or non-professional athletes within the official context of the sport system and its organisations. Their activities focus on preparing and winning sport events such as races, meetings, and championships.
- Amateur sport is still carried out within sport organisations. In addition to performing, it encompasses further goals such as fitness, health, socialising, education, or integration. Formal or informal competitions may be more or less relevant events for amateur athletes.
- Leisure sport is not necessarily coupled to organisations. It can be formal or informal and is a voluntary, non-binding, recreational physical activity, which to a certain degree is inspired by sport.

34 Systems Theoretical Framework

It can be practised in a game-like form of (informal) competition or can be centred on other goals.

This categorisation by no means implies a hierarchy but is rather a separated (albeit partly overlapping) and horizontal heterogeneity (Stichweh, 1990). While other function systems tend to disembody the individual, the body is central in the sport system and all its subfields. Simple explanations of the emergence of sport as compensation for the loss of the body in modern times are neglected. And yet, according to Bette (1989), the paradoxical simultaneity of physical distancing and physical enhancement is a plausible explanation of the relevance of sport in our society.

Outside systems theory, it has been noted that the corporality (*zoe*) of refugees plays a key role in the examination of their status, which is stripped of the social dimension of life (*bios*) (1998). This research does not consider this convergence to be casual and instead treats it as one specific connection between experiences of sport and forced migration: perhaps sport nourishes a physicality that characterises refugees' bare life. Thereby, the body, the satisfaction of its needs (Maslow, 1943), and the preservation of its deriving capital (Wacquant, 1995) are some of the remaining fixed points and achievable goals for them at certain points in their lives.

5.1.3 Typification of the considered systems

The profound implications of Luhmann's typology of systems indubitably calls for further clarification. Nevertheless, the brief explanation contained in the section above is sufficient to typify the systems that lie at the core of each of the four projects. This typification is a necessary reduction of complexity because the phenomenon needs to first be divided into smaller and simpler and therefore observable phenomena. However, the initial accentuation and focus is only one step in the research process. After examining these facets separately, this book will deliver a complexity-appropriate description by taking all different levels into account. Because other interpretations are possible, the section below proposes one way[4] of understanding the types of systems underlying each project included in this research:

- *Sport and Forced Migration in the Mass Media* focuses primarily on society. In this project, newspapers embody the mass media's perspective. In other words, it examines the selective observation of the topic through the logic of a function system. According to

Luhmann (2000, p. 2), mass media are 'all those institutions of society which make use of copying technologies to disseminate communication'. The basic code of this system is the distinction 'information/non-information' (Luhmann, 2000, p. 17). Information is the positive value that describes the possibilities of this system's operations. Nevertheless, the function of mass media is the social memory generated by the totality of this information and not the information itself (Luhmann, 2000, p. 65). Mass media observe their environment, make a productive selection of newsworthy information and broadcast it. This information can be received by anyone, yet any sender-receiver interaction in the presence of both is excluded. In the 21st century, mass media are characterised by the development of communication technologies that allow for wide and rapid dissemination of communication and by the establishment of internally differentiated areas of programming, which include news, reports, entertainment, and advertising (Luhmann, 2000, p. 24).

- *Activities for Refugees in Sports Clubs* examines organisations' interactions between sports clubs' human resources and refugee participants in sport offers. In principle, this chapter considers a special type of organisation in relation to the topic forced migration and sport. Sports clubs are formal organisations whose operation is primarily oriented towards the sport system's code of 'victory/defeat' (Schimank, 1988). As organisations are fertile grounds for structural couplings (Luhmann, 2018), sports clubs do not only follow this particular logic but may also pursue other goals, such as the promotion of health, education, and social inclusion. Organisations are *autopoietic* social systems consisting of and being reproduced through (communicated) decisions (Luhmann, 2006). All of their features are the results of preceding organisational decisions and are based on certain premises (Luhmann, 2006; Thiel & Mayer, 2009). Systems theoretical literature traditionally focuses on the following decision premises (Luhmann, 2006; Thiel & Mayer, 2009; Thiel & Meier, 2004): decision programmes define the organisation's goals and how to achieve them. Communication channels are horizontal and vertical divisions of tasks, hierarchies, and assignments of responsibilities concerning work processes. Human resources refers to how individuals are assigned to different areas of action and responsibility by identifying and matching their qualifications. Moreover, the culture of an organisation, even though it may be implicit, influences all of the organisation's decision-making processes.

- Similarly, *Physical Activity in Refugee Sites* examines both interactions and organisations. However, it also presents a contrasting organisational perspective. It examines how a humanitarian organisation that is specialised in the management of forced migration (Malkki, 1995) and its human resources understand sport as an activity specifically designed for the residents of refugee sites. As an example of a refugee site, this project considers the ETM of Niamey as an organisation that provides shelter and meals for its residents while creating legal possibilities to manage their re-inclusion in society. The decisions of a refugee site are guided by a mix of systemic logics (Luhmann, 2006; Roth & Schutz, 2015), which include legal (legal/illegal), political (inferior/superior power), and moral logics (right/wrong). However, its decisions are not only led by structural couplings between these sometimes contradictory logics but also by the state of emergency, the scarcity of resources and the direct involvement of many organisations, among which UNHCR is by far the most influential. Consequently, a refugee site is a complex organisation that mobilises many people and resources.
- Finally, *Forced Migration and Elite Sport* explores athletes or rather individuals' roles in relation to function systems and organisations. Despite concentrating on individuals, the biographical focus only considers interactions superficially, for example those between a coach and an athlete. Therefore, this project examines the role of individuals within function systems and organisations. Importantly, individuals do not constitute social systems but are included on the basis of specific roles in diverse social systems (Luhmann, 2005). At the elite level, sport organisations include individuals as athletes amongst other specific roles (Schimank, 1988, p. 85). Elite-level athletes have reached the highest levels of competition (Delaney & Madigan, 2009, p. 94), are hyper included in sport (Bette & Gugutzer, 2012) and are required to win (Bette & Kutsch, 1981): the athlete must achieve successes within a relatively short period of time (active career), take high risks (amongst others, risk of injury), and faces ruthlessly competitive rules. With the exception of illegal means for improving performance (for example, doping), the sport system ignores any factor within an athlete's sport career which may impede or enhance his or her performances (Stichweh, 1990), including forced migration.

5.2 Other theories

While this book adopts a systems theoretical perspective, some of the articles included here rely on post-structuralism and socialisation theory. These theories were deemed good alternatives for examining specific aspects of the social phenomenon at hand and will be briefly outlined below.

Foucault's theory is used to expose and explain the production and legitimisation of dominance through the concept of discourse. From this perspective, 'discourse' is a system of thoughts composed of ideas, attitudes, beliefs, and practices that systematically construct the world and its subjects (Foucault, 1972; Lessa, 2006). It is not a language but rather a practice or an ideology because it provides a systematic way of thinking about a topic (J.R. Martin, 2015, p. 54). Discourses are embedded in wider social processes of domination, subjectification and knowledge production. There is broad agreement amongst scholars that issues of power affect mass media (Andrews, 1993; Cole et al., 2004; Markula & Pringle, 2006; Rail & Harvey, 1995), sport (Chauzy & Appave, 2013; Cooper et al., 2017; Eberl et al., 2018), and their intersections. Moreover, the Foucauldian theory (1977) was partly applied to the study of refugee sites. From this perspective, together with prisons, schools, hospitals, and military barracks, refugee sites are a place where technological disciplinary powers apply. They are a relatively recent form of disciplinary institution, and became a key tool in the management of the 'refugee crisis'. Refugee sites are exposed to a continuous and 'unequal gaze', allowing for an almost constant observation arising from the involvement of many agencies with different aims in this setting. This creates a situation of 'gentle' punishment, which is prison-like, even though refugees did not commit any crime aside from having escaped a dangerous situation.

Hurrelmann's interactional version of socialisation theory (1988) was applied to the study of refugee athletes' sport careers. Socialisation is understood as the process of emergence, formation, and development of personality through the reciprocal interaction between the human organism and the social and ecological environment (Hurrelmann, 1988). Personality is the specific and uniquely organised structure of an individual's motives, characteristics, attitudes, and dispositions. The lifelong productive processing of reality relies on the availability of personal and social resources for coping with the environment. Psychophysical dispositions constitute the internal reality, whereas the social and ecological environment constitute the external reality, which are both subjective perceptions in a constructivist sense.

This basic but tailored framework and its applications to research on athletes with a migration background (Burrmann et al., 2017; Burrmann et al., 2015a; Zender, 2018) provide a fruitful theoretical foundation for a biography-based examination of the reciprocal influences between sport socialisation and forced migration.

Notes

1 For example, those conceived by Bertalanffy (1968) and Parsons (1951).
2 Europe is generally accorded the status of a full continent, which comprises the western-most part of Eurasia and is bordered by seas to the north, west, and the south, and by Asia to the east. The Ural Mountains, the Ural River, the Caspian Sea, the Greater Caucasus, the Black Sea, and the waterways of Turkey are commonly considered as separating Europe from Asia (National Geographic Society, 1999).
3 While this term is more appropriate for a system's theory-based sociological analysis, irritation can be translated with the more intuitive term 'influence'.
4 Different interpretations are possible against the backdrop and epistemological position and features of systems in systems theory. Moreover, social phenomena exist within different systems and the focus of the research sometimes switches across different types of systems.

6 Methodical Approaches of the Projects

Each of the habilitation's projects examines a different aspect of the topic *forced migration and sport* using a distinct empirical approach. Table 6.1 presents the mix of qualitative methods applied by the respective projects to the collection of data, the creation of data sets, and to their analysis.

Methodologically, this study is located in the field of qualitative research (Lloyd, 2000). The methods applied (interviews, observations, and document analysis) are a systematic means to carry out basic human techniques to create knowledge: listening, observing, and reading (Gobo, 2018, p. 80). This section covers a non-exhaustive catalogue of approaches and studies that constitute the main references for developing the specific methodological design of each individual project. Primary data were mostly collected through narrative (Schütze, 1983) or expert (Gläser & Laudel, 2010) interviews and participant or non-participant observations (Spradley, 2016). Document analysis (Bowen, 2009) was the method applied to complement the information gathered through the other approaches or used as a standalone qualitative research method. In some cases, these three methods were applied separately and in other cases, they constituted approaches for carrying out ethnographic research (Hammersley & Atkinson, 2019).

The data created through these methods consist of transcriptions, field notes and diaries, and document collections. The raw interview data were refined by transcribing them in accordance with the rules of *Talk in Qualitative Research* (Bohnsack et al., 2013) or in a more plain form. The observations were logged (sometimes via paper-and-pencil first) in different forms of field notes or diaries, which were based on principles of ethnography (Hammersley & Atkinson, 2019). The catalogue of newspaper articles was constructed following loose guidelines for media analyses (Witten et al., 2010). The data analysis applied

Table 6.1 Methodological approaches of the habilitation

Project	Data Collection	Data Set	Analysis
Sport and Forced Migration in the Mass Media (Germany)	Creation of a catalogue of articles from German newspapers on the topic 'forced migration and sport'	1,840 articles published in German newspapers	Qualitative content analysis and discourse analysis
Activities for Refugees in Sports Clubs (Germany)	Interviews (28+7); participant and non-participant observations (30h); collection of project reports (29)	Interview transcriptions (28+7); observation protocols (7); projects' documents (29)	Qualitative content analysis and thematic analysis
Physical Activity in Refugee Sites (Niger)	Participant and non-participant observations (120h); interviews (10); collection of information	Transcriptions of interviews (10); field diary; news and UNHCR's documents	Qualitative content analysis
Forced Migration and Elite Sport (Europe)	Participant and non-participant observations (500h); interviews (21); collection of information	Transcriptions of interviews (21); field notes; news and social media posts	Qualitative content analysis and documentary method

Methodical Approaches of the Projects 41

techniques of qualitative document analysis (Mayring, 2015), thematic analysis (V. Braun & Clarke, 2012), template analysis (V. Braun & Clarke, 2012), discourse analysis (Wodak & Meyer, 2001), and the documentary method (Bohnsack et al., 2013). The next sections explain the methodological approaches of each of the research projects in more detail.

6.1 Researching mass media

To explore the mass media's representation of sport in the context of the 'refugee crisis', a 'corpus of statements' was established. This catalogue was created by aggregating articles published in German newspapers on the topic *forced migration and sport* between 2013 and 2018. To create a relevant catalogue, the four most widely circulated newspapers were selected (Statista, 2020b), namely Bild, Sueddeutsche Zeitung (SZ), Die Welt (Welt), and Frankfurter Allgemeine Zeitung (FAZ). They represent different viewpoints within the national German print media landscape (Koopmans & Pfetsch, 2007, p. 70): a tabloid paper (Bild), a centre-left (SZ), a centre-right (FAZ), as well as a 'liberal-cosmopolitan' to conservative newspaper (Welt). To ensure consistent and representative sampling, relevant news on the topic *forced migration and sport* was selected through a systematic search in the electronic database FACTIVA and in the FAZ archive. A research team carried out the search between 2018 and 2019. The electronic databases were explored using the search function for one or more terms related to sport ('physical activity', 'sport', 'exercise', 'training') combined with at least one term related to refugees ('refugee', 'migration', 'escape', 'forced migration', 'migrant', 'CALD').[1] All articles were issued between 1 January 2013 and 31 December 2018 in the selected newspapers, and contained the above-mentioned keywords related to *forced migration and sport*.

Figure 6.1 presents the three selection steps of this search, which refined the 22,041 hits generated during the initial rough search without the use of filters. A successive refinement of the search through the application of filters to the databases enabled a narrowing down of hits to 12,230. Following this first refinement, there were still too many hits because many articles (particularly those published before the peak of the 'refugee crisis' in 2015) focused on migrants, not refugees. To reduce the catalogue to exclusively contain articles on refugees, the articles' title, headline, and occasionally their content had to be read. In its final version, the catalogue comprised 1,840 articles.

42 Methodical Approaches of the Projects

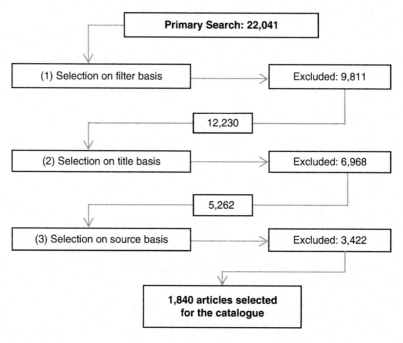

Figure 6.1 Selection of relevant articles. As a first analytical step, all articles were distributed according to time and newspaper (see Table 6.2).[2]

Table 6.2 Distribution of articles on *forced migration and sport*

	Bild	Sueddeutsche Zeitung	Die Welt	Frankfurter Allgemeine Zeitung	Total
2013	2	40	2	4	48
2014	17	115	10	15	157
2015	190	420	46	106	762
2016	131	218	42	83	474
2017	37	83	23	33	176
2018	51	95	39	38	223
Total	428	971	162	279	1,840

This catalogue was analysed using a Foucauldian-inspired discourse analysis (Arribas-Ayllon & Walkerdine, 2008; Tannen et al., 2015), which is a form of discourse analysis based on the theories of Michel Foucault aimed at raising critique. That is, this project analysed material generated by mass media with the goal of exposing and explaining how dominance is reproduced and legitimated. Amongst other limitations that generally apply to qualitative (Kuckartz & Rädiker, 2019) and discourse analysis (Tannen et al., 2015), the depth of this study was limited by the quantity of material analysed (Baker et al., 2008).

6.2 Researching sport organisations

To review sports clubs in the context of the 'refugee crisis', a research team of the TU Dortmund and of the University of Münster examined different sport offers supported by the national programme 'Orientation through Sport' (OtS) between 2016 and 2017. OtS is an ongoing programme financed by the German Federal Government and implemented by the youth section of the German Olympic Sports Confederation (dsj). It financially supports, amongst others, the establishment of sport offers for young, unaccompanied refugees (dsj, 2020). Both sport federations and clubs provide these offers nationwide. The goal of this project was to explore how sports clubs organised offers for refugees using a mix of qualitative methods. This included an analysis of (29) applications and reports produced by the clubs, (28) telephone interviews with persons responsible for the sport offers, and (7) participant observations of selected sport activities. Additionally, the seven clubs previously visited were re-contacted in 2019 for a follow-up telephone interview. This allowed for a consideration of the development of the selected sport offers and thus their longitudinal development. Finally, the interviews conducted in the context of this study were merged with the empirical material of two other two research projects: *Sport for and with Refugees* (SfwR) and *Refugee Work of Sport Clubs* (RWfSC).[3] Thereby, a broader catalogue of semi-structured qualitative interviews (n = 49) with people directly or indirectly responsible for sport activities targeted at refugees in German sports clubs was created. Table 6.3 contains details on the type of activities offered within the sport programmes discussed in a selection of interviews with contact persons (CP) in the different sports clubs.

These qualitative data entail various aspects of the sport offers from the perspective of the clubs' volunteers and were analysed using different approaches to content analysis (V. Braun & Clarke, 2012). Specific aspects of this topic were explored from the perspective of systems theory (Michelini et al., 2018), from an organisational capacity perspective (Tuchel et al., 2021) and through a realistic evaluation approach (Michelini & Burrmann, 2021).

Table 6.3 Catalogue of interviews in sports clubs

List of Interviews OtS		List of Interviews SfwR	
CP	Type of Sport	CP	Type of Sport
1	Various sport activities	12	Various sport activities
3	Cricket	14	Martial arts
4	Football	17	Football
6	Football, running	18	Football
7	Gymnastics	23	Various sport activities
8	Various sport activities	24	Floorball
9	Various sport activities	25	Various sport activities
10	Table tennis	26	Various sport activities
11	Various sport activities	27	Various sport activities
12	Canoeing	30	Various sport activities
13	Football		
14	Various sport activities	\multicolumn{2}{l}{List of Interviews RWfSC}
15	Rowing	3	Martial arts
16	Various sport activities	4	Football
17	Various sport activities	5	Football
18	Bike-riding	6	Football
19	Various sport activities	7	Various sport activities
20	Various sport activities	8	Various sport activities
22	Various sport activities	9	Various sport activities
23	Various sport activities	10	Martial arts
24	Various sport activities	11	Cricket
25	Climbing groups	13	Football
26	Various sport activities	14	Various sport activities
27	Various sport activities	15	Table tennis
28	Climbing	16	Various sport activities
		17	Football

The sample exclusively consisted of sports clubs that organised sport offers for refugees and may therefore be particularly open and integrative. Moreover, despite the quantity and quality of its data and successive extensions, this project mostly ignored the perspective of participants who were only partially considered in participant observations. The triangulation (Flick, 2011) of data was limited by the low quality and sometimes even absence of organisations' reports and by the small number of participant observations.

6.3 Researching refugee sites

This ongoing project aims to understand the role of sport in refugee sites.[4] While this implies exploring and comparing sport activities in a relevant sample of refugee sites around the world, the current state of this research is limited to the cross-sectional examination of one case study outside Europe. The COVID-19 pandemic prevented further visits to this specific and to other sites. This chapter therefore considers sport within the scope of UNHCR's Emergency Transit Mechanism (ETM) of Niamey (Niger) based on data gathered in 2019. The research was carried out using ethnographic methods (Jackson, 2017). According to the ethical recommendations of the TU Dortmund's ethics commission, which endorsed the methodology and scope of this study, the author directly participated in all of the research activities, clearly stating his role as a sociologist and the goals of the study.

During a four-week research period, around 120 hours of ethnographic activities at the ETM's sites were carried out. These activities included observations, interviews and natural forms of data collection. Approximately 60 hours of participant observations were spent actively taking part in sport activities with refugees, some of these hours as one of the coaches in a football-based project (20 hours) and the rest (40 hours) as an active participant in other sport offers at the sites (swimming and Taekwondo). The remaining 60 hours were spent at the ETM before and after participation in these activities. Interviews were also a relevant source of information. Ten narrative interviews focused on sport in the refugee sites of Niamey and were conducted with staff working at the sites. The interviewees were three interpreters with a refugee background, four managers of UNHCR with European roots and three trainers from Niger. Each of the interviews lasted around one hour and were carried out formally on appointment after having informed the participant about the objectives of the interview and obtaining his/her consent (Table 6.4).

Table 6.4 Catalogue of interviews in Niamey's refugee sites

Interviewee	Language	Nationality	Sex
Interpreter 1	English	Somali	Male
Interpreter 2	English	Somali	Male
Interpreter 3	English	Somali	Male
Manager 1	Italian	Italian	Female
Manager 2	Italian	Italian	Female
Manager 3	Italian	Italian	Female
Manager 4	English	Italian	Male
Trainer 1	French	Nigerien	Male
Trainer 2	English	Nigerien	Male
Trainer 3	French	Nigerien	Male

Finally, information during non-working and informal situations was also collected and summarised. This method of natural data collection included situations before, during and after working hours, such as talks, individual answers to specific questions and casual chats with refugees and with people working at the sites. This material also included summaries of experiences with free time, conversations, news articles and impressions, which contributed supplementary sources to the aim of the research.

This material comprised 50 pages of daily written notes in the form of a field diary. After the visit, the diary was integrated and adjusted, but not reworked or interpreted. The field diary was used as a basis for analysis, reflection and interpretation. The components of the data set were examined using content analysis techniques (Krippendorff, 2013) and interpreted in the systems theoretical tradition (see Luhmann, 1997, pp. 36–41). This allowed for a sociological observation of the role of sport in creating and solving the problem of managing mass displacement.

Besides the limitations of ethnography in general (Hammersley & Atkinson, 2019), the specific methodological limitations of this ethnographic project included insufficient time of fieldwork and the consideration of only one refugee site. Moreover, the foreign appearance and overt identity of the researcher constituted a problem for the ecological validity of the study (Mapedzahama & Dune, 2017). Language represented a further challenge because the author could not properly follow many situations, although the possibility to rely on interpreters and translators was provided on occasion. Finally, the sites' staff became the most important source of information for this research project while refugees were a less accessible source for data.

6.4 Researching refugee athletes

This longitudinal (2016–2018) project examined the sport socialisation of a group of (former) elite Syrian water polo players, who found asylum in different European countries. In accordance with methodological and theoretical aspects, this project was carried out through multi-sited ethnography (Marcus, 1995).

The project 'Forced Migration and Elite Sport' developed by chance. The author met Monzer[5] after he had fled from Syria to Dortmund (Germany) in 2016. Monzer wanted to start playing water polo again after his forced migration and contacted the water polo team the author played for between 2013 and 2020. He provided the first biographical

Methodical Approaches of the Projects 47

Table 6.5 Sample of Forced Migration and Elite Sport

Name[6]	Age	Country	Resettled	Sport Participation (2016–2018)[7]
Hossam	51	Sweden	2014	Coach and referee
Ramzin	42	Sweden	2015	1st and 2nd division
Lorans	24	Holland	2014	1st and 2nd division
Mufed	26	Sweden	2012	1st and 2nd division
Monzer	24	Germany	2015	4th and 5th division
Jamal	22	Sweden	2015	Inactive
Aman	24	Germany	2011	Inactive

interview for this project and acted as a gatekeeper, introducing other Syrian water polo players who had resettled in Europe to the author. This project gradually developed as a longitudinal and multi-sided ethnographic project with seven participants (Table 6.5).

The material for this research study was collected through overt ethnography (Hammersley & Atkinson, 2019). In quantitative terms, the author spent about 500 hours in situations in which most of the sample was together. Additional time was spent with individual participants, especially with Monzer, with whom the author shared a substantial amount of time. Data collection was based on interviews and participative observations:

- Each respondent participated in a long (90 minutes) biographical-centred interview in 2016 and two shorter (45 minutes) follow-up interviews in 2017 and 2018. The first two were face-to-face interviews conducted during water polo tournaments, and the last one was carried out via Skype. The 21 interviews were conducted by the author in a foreign language for both himself and the interviewees (English or German).
- The author accompanied the subjects to three water polo tournaments, participated with them actively and passively in training camps and visited the individuals included in the sample every year between 2016 and 2018. About 100 pages of manually written field notes summarised these participant and non-participant observations.

By asking, observing, and reading (Gobo, 2018), material was created in form of transcriptions (interviews) and field notes (observations) and was complemented with secondary sources (documents). Qualitative content analysis (Schreier, 2014) and the documentary method (Bohnsack et al., 2013) were applied to these data, as systematic and flexible empirical methods to examine the meaning behind data. The material was initially interpreted through the interactional concept of socialisation theory (Hurrelmann, 1988) and is re-interpreted here through Luhmann's systems theory.

The strengths of the project are its focus on the experiences of refugees (Kohli, 2006) and its longitudinal design. In addition to the limitations of ethnography (Hammersley & Atkinson, 2019), the close relationship between the author and the sample, the sometimes chaotic context of the interviews and the long breaks between the research events limit the quality of the data.

Notes

1 These search terms were chosen based on their relevance to the articles' topic and based on the lexicon of previously examined research on forced migration and sport. Within the search string, the keywords within the two groups were connected with the word 'OR' and the two groups were connected with the word 'AND'. In the original German version, this string was: (*körperliche Aktivität* OR *Übung* OR *Training* OR *Sport* OR *Sportler*) AND (*Flüchtling* OR *Flucht* OR *Migration* OR *Migrant* OR *Zwangsmigration*).
2 This catalogue of articles was extended or integrated with additional document types to analyse the cases of two refugee elite athletes (Yusra Mardini and Bakery Jatta).
3 These are briefly presented below:

- The research project SfwR was carried out by the Technical University of Chemnitz and aimed *inter alia* at describing the actual state of sport-related refugee work in the city of Chemnitz (Saxony) by focusing on the potential, deficits, and best practices of sport offers in local VSCs. The material of this project that was analysed encompassed 10 semi-structured interviews conducted with the persons responsible for the sport offers.
- The research project RWfSC was part of a larger research cluster on forced migration and solidarity carried out by the Humboldt University of Berlin. It analysed motives, practices, and challenges of sports clubs that focus on the integration of refugees in Berlin and in Saxony. The material of this project that was analysed included 14 interviews with board members and coaches responsible for sport offers.

4 This text uses the word 'site' instead of camp to indicate a wider range of settlements, which include but are not limited to camps.
5 To protect the privacy of the respondents, this book replaces names with pseudonyms and removes some of the geographical indications.

Methodical Approaches of the Projects 49

6 In addition to the common sport background, family relationships characterised part of the sample: Hossam is the father of Mufed; Monzer and Aman are brothers; Jamal and Ramzin are distant relatives of Hossam's family. Hossam, Ramzin, Mufed, and Jamal live close to each other, just like Monzer and Aman.

7 The overall prevalence of water polo in Sweden is lower than in Germany and Holland. Because of the scarcity of tradition and clubs, the Swedish first league is still an amateur competition.

7 Results of the Projects

This chapter presents the results of the four individual research projects. Each examines a different aspect of the overall topic *forced migration and sport*. The results are summarised and supplemented through further unpublished material, which already existed or was developed for this research. Table 7.1 presents the published, accepted or at least submitted articles on the projects' results to peer reviewed scientific journals.[1]

The following sections briefly present the main results of each research project. The description comprises a short synthesis and theoretical interpretation of the projects' outcomes, which the reader can further deepen by reading the related articles at the end of each section.

7.1 Sport and forced migration in the mass media

The first project explores the question 'How do mass media represent sport in the context of the "refugee crisis"?' by examining a catalogue of articles published in German newspapers.

It builds on existing studies on the German press's representation of the refugee crisis (Akpınar & Wagner, 2019; Engel et al., 2019; Holmes & Castañeda, 2016; Holzberg et al., 2018; Vollmer & Karakayali, 2018). The radical constructivist epistemological position of sociological systems theory implies that reality is always constructed through observation. Notably, mass media mirrors and influences social expectations and attitudes towards specific events, situations or circumstances (Richardson, 2006, p. 1). Therefore, the scientific examination of sport-related topics within mass media representation of the 'refugee crisis' is scientifically relevant.

This project focused on newspapers, i.e. on publicly accessible, periodical publications containing information on a broad range of current events (Faulstich, 2000). While newspapers have traditionally

DOI: 10.4324/9781003370673-7

Table 7.1 Research projects and scientific articles

Projects	Articles
Sport and Forced Migration in the Mass Media	Michelini, E., & Seiberth, K. (2022). Refugee, Footballer and (Anti-)Hero: The Case of Bakery Jatta. A Discourse Analysis of German Newspapers. *Soccer and Society*.
	Michelini, E. (2021). The Representation of the 'Refugee Crisis' and 'Sport' in the German Press: An Analysis of Newspaper Discourse. *European Journal for Sport and Society*.
	Michelini, E. (2021). The Representation of Yusra Mardini as a Refugee Olympic Athlete: A Sociological Analysis. *Sport und Gesellschaft*.
Activities for Refugees in Sports Clubs	Michelini, E., et al. (2018). Sport Offers for Refugees in Germany. Promoting and Hindering Conditions in Voluntary Sport Clubs. *Society Register*.
	Tuchel, J., et al. (2021). Practices of Voluntary Sports Clubs to Include Refugees. *Sport in Society*.
	Burrmann, U., & Michelini, E. (2021). A Preliminary Impact Model for the Integration of Young Refugees through Sport Programmes. *Culture e Studi del Sociale*.
Physical Activity in Refugee Sites	Michelini, E. (2022). Organised Sport in Refugee Sites: An Ethnographic Research in Niamey. *European Journal for Sport and Society*.
Forced Migration and Elite Sport	Michelini, E. (2018). War, Migration, Resettlement and Sport Socialization of Young Athletes: The Case of Syrian Elite Water Polo. *European Journal for Sport and Society*.
	Michelini, E. (2020). Coping with Sport Ambitions after Forced Migration: Strategies of Refugee Athletes. *European Journal for Sport and Society*.
	Michelini, E. (2020-Submitted). The Relevance of Sport in the Lives of Refugee Athletes after their Resettlement. *Z'Flucht*.

52 *Results of the Projects*

been printed, most of them today are also or exclusively published online. The acquisition and dissemination of information is subject to universally applicable journalistic ethics and standards, which include the principles of truthfulness, accuracy, objectivity, impartiality, fairness, and public accountability (International Federation of Journalists, 2019). However, newspapers' reporting differs considerably in terms of frequency, geographical scope and distribution, subject matter and technology. Finally, as they are produced by an organisation, newspapers' reporting also emerges as a communicative product of decision premises (Luhmann, 2000), such as human resources (notably by an editor, journalists and a circulation department), programmes (amongst others, the organisation's mission and vision) and communication structures (hierarchy and management style).

Alone a simple observation of the articles' distribution over time provides some initial interesting 'quantitative' information. Notably, the number of articles published on the topic *forced migration and sport* increased during the peak of the 'refugee crisis' between 2015 and 2016, and decreased thereafter. This trend is visible in Figure 7.1, with the grey line depicting the number of asylum applications (in thousand; modified from Statista, 2020a) and the black line representing the number of articles published in Germany between 2013 and 2018.

The fact that the quantitative peak of articles slightly anticipates that of asylum applications could be explained by the topic's stronger newsworthiness (Boyd, 1994; Luhmann, 2000), when the phenomenon was still evolving and was to some extent unpredictable. Another possible or concurring explanation is saturation and the consequent loss of interest in the topic after the peak had been reached (Heslop, 2016).

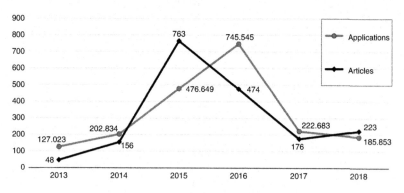

Figure 7.1 Asylum applications and articles in Germany.

Table 7.2 Distribution of articles per year and category

Category Year	Athletes	Criminality	Engagement	Housing	Integration	Resources	Total
2013	9	3	–	19	16	1	48
2014	7	9	48	54	15	23	156
2015	23	27	54	359	213	87	763
2016	83	27	28	137	159	40	474
2017	26	9	16	16	87	22	176
2018	76	22	38	18	60	9	223
Total	224	97	184	603	550	182	1,840

Table 7.2 provides a general overview of the topics of all newspaper articles in each considered year. These six categories emerged inductively and were classified and grouped on the basis of their main theme.[2] These categories are briefly described as follows:[3]

1 Athletes: this theme focused on the sport careers of athletes with a refugee background. Articles on refugee or migrant athletes were also included if they had a direct reference to the 'refugee crisis'.
2 Criminality: this theme focused on crimes against or committed by refugees. Sport was sometimes a setting (sports halls or facilities), a context (matches or training sessions) or an object (theft or damage) of these acts.
3 Engagement: this theme referred to internal and external perceptions of sport systems' engagement in the context of the 'refugee crisis' at different societal levels.
4 Housing: the most frequent theme covered in the articles concerned the accommodation of refugees in sport facilities, principally in the sports halls of clubs and schools.
5 Integration: during the 'refugee crisis', integration was a major political topic that resonated in sport-related press reports.
6 Resources: this category entailed the mobilisation and distribution of economic resources for refugees in the context of sport.

The catalogue was embedded in previously existing debates on the 'refugee crisis' (Eberl et al., 2018) and on the integrative power of sport (Smith et al., 2019). Regardless of the close relationship between sport and the mass media (Stichweh, 2018), the existence of this consistent reporting indicates the newsworthiness of sport-related topics in the context of the 'refugee crisis'. The fact that many articles were published suggests that the topics introduced above satisfied sufficient criteria to be selected for dissemination, in particular as regards the selectors: surprise, conflicts, local relevance, norm violations, moral judgment, personification, and topicality (Luhmann, 2000). How newspapers report an event is highly relevant, because the description of a social phenomenon limits its contingency and shapes its social expectation. Moreover, in the case of sport, the construction of a critical situation served as a self-fulfilling prophecy (Luhmann, 1984a) and created feelings of uncertainty, discomfort, and fear. For example, the alarmist tone of the information on the use of sport facilities as shelters for refugees raised preoccupations about the impossibility of offering the standard programmes of sports clubs and physical education lessons. In retrospect, the intense discussions on this topic overestimated the problem, which was rapidly resolved through the creation of new reception centres.[4]

7.2 Activities for refugees in sports clubs

The second project addressed the question 'How do sports clubs organise sport activities for refugees?' based on data collected in the scientific supervision of 'Orientation through Sport' (OtS).

Sports clubs are organisations that are primarily coupled with the sport system but also with other function systems and embedded in society as a whole. As a relevant irritation, the 'refugee crisis' is supposed to foster change in the autopoietic operations of sports clubs (Figure 7.2).

With about 90,000 organisations and 28 million members, sports clubs are widespread in Germany (S. Braun & Nobis, 2011). Research on German sports clubs reveals that 18.2 per cent of all organisations provided special offers for refugees at the height of the 'refugee crisis' (Breuer, 2017, p. 69). Despite indications of an overestimation of their alleged integrative potential (Dowling, 2020; Seiberth & Thiel, 2010; Seiberth et al., 2013), sports clubs were continuously perceived and perceived themselves as relevant integrative settings for refugees (Block & Gibbs, 2017). Apart from the author's analysis, the adaptation of sports clubs to the 'refugee crisis' was also swiftly and thoroughly examined by the German scientific community (Feuchter & Janetzko, 2018; Michelini et al., 2018; Nowy et al., 2020; Seiberth et al., 2018; Tuchel et al., 2021; Verweyen, 2019).

According to the results of this project (Table 7.3), the conditions that promote and obstruct the implementation of sport offers for refugees were identified in all formal (decision programmes, communication channels and human resources) and informal (organisational culture) decision premises (Michelini et al., 2018).

Results of the Projects 55

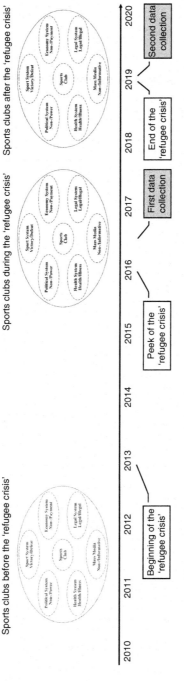

Figure 7.2 Impact of the 'refugee crisis' on sports clubs.

Table 7.3 Conditions for refugee-specific sport programmes

Decision Premise	Promoting	Hindering
Decision programmes	Existence of integration as a goal in purpose programmes and of previous integrative sport offers; guidelines to lead the implementation and evaluation of integrative programmes	Absence of integration as a goal in purpose programmes and of previous integrative sport offers
Communication channels	Low veto potential through clubs' communicative structures; information oligarchies pro integration	Non-existent or only formally existing posts for integration
Human resources	High engagement for refugees by persons working in the sports club	Exclusion of refugees from working in the sports clubs
Organisational culture	Integrative culture; changing capacity; positive external influence; welcoming culture	Non-integrative culture; resistance to change; negative external influence; stereotypes

Despite the broad diffusion of these conditions, human resources play a central and decisive role. Indeed, as other studies suggest (Seiberth et al., 2018), the resolute determination of individuals or of small groups of people was highly relevant for the implementation of these offers.

CP: *This was all run through me, I thought it's important. I can do this within my job and I am the contact person, and all this was part of my position. I think it's important to have a central contact point and that it's not divided among 2, 3, 4 persons. Of course, you're always in contact with your cooperation partners, your paid workers – whoever is on site. But everything was directly run through me. I wrote the application and was in charge of project coordination, -planning, -implementation, etc.* (OtS-17: Lines 29–30)

Surprisingly, when it comes to organising sport offers for refugees, sport organisations display an unexpected dynamic and high capacity to rapidly mobilise resources. This might be the reason why a general feeling of being overwhelmed and an immediate sense of frustration in case of negative experiences and drawbacks was reported by the interview partners. Sports clubs almost unanimously organised sport offers free of charge as an effective way to lower the entry barriers for refugees.

I: *What about compulsory insurance or membership fees?*
CP: *They didn't have to pay. It was free for refugees. And there were offers for refugees to participate in some sort of an apprenticeship to train others.* (OtS-18: Lines 51–52)

However, it was also observed in one or the other case that users tended to underestimate the value of free sport offers (Mohammadi, 2019).

The project's findings also show that sports clubs often developed unconventional practices in response to the 'refugee crisis' (Tuchel et al., 2021). The following practices to make sport offers accessible to refugees were identified: sports clubs collaborated with other organisations to implement sport offers in refugee reception sites; refugees could participate in regular club offers, often free of charge; and 'refugee sport groups' were created, which engaged in sport separately from other training groups.

CP: *We immediately, when refugees came to [location], we immediately went there and made offers. "Guys, you can join us and engage in sports". Children from the entire region, around 14, were part of a soccer group, boys and girls mixed, it was amazing. Then, unfortunately, the gym where these sport offers were taking place, was taken from us. We continued providing sport offers, but not for this group, which disbanded. But we have fitness groups that are part of a running group. We tried to engage in as much sport with refugees as possible, but it wasn't easy to reach the refugees, that's the big problem, because for the operators, it's only an 8 to 4 job.* (RWoSC-7: Line 31)

Finally, the relationships between the context factors, mechanisms and outcomes of the OtS programme were explored through a realistic evaluation. To this end, the data collected for this project were considered against beliefs about the integration potential attributed to organised sport and previous findings on the integration effects of sports clubs for migrants, especially for young refugees. Focusing on the sport offers' social integration goals, a preliminary impact model was developed (Michelini & Burrmann, 2021). The longitudinal data on the programmes show that a consolidation and expansion of the sports programmes occurred over time. In some cases, however, the clubs had to modify their plans to manage the activities' continuation and few of them were dismissed. Despite good conditions, joint events (e.g. weekend excursions) and committed volunteers, some contact persons stated that the development of relationships between the refugees and the members of the sports clubs outside the special activities was scarce. Presumably, three years was not enough and more time would have been needed.

CP: *So I don't see it coming, that they [the refugee groups] will automatically integrate into already existing groups. Some play table tennis, others play volleyball. Nevertheless, we also communicate this and repeatedly inform all departments about the fact that we also have funding for this, but this does not mean their attitude changes. Or even their own goals in their departments. We tend to set these goals in our working group.*
(OtS-18: Line 7)

From a systems theoretical perspective, this analysis reveals that the 'refugee crisis' was an event that had an impact on society as a whole, its systems and its sports clubs. While the staff of sports clubs included here showed a surprising level of enthusiasm and dynamism and adequate financial support was mostly available, the implementation of programmes for refugees has been difficult and overwhelming. Changes in the social attitude towards refugees, the constraints of organisational dynamics, and a gradual loss of enthusiasm or even a gradual de-sensitisation and de-motivation may be explanations for this feeling of fatigue and frustration.[5]

7.3 Physical activity in refugee sites

The third project explored the topic *forced migration and sport* within the setting of refugee sites. The project's scientific basis (Michelini, 2022) focuses on the question 'How do refugee sites organise sport activities for refugees?'

Contrary to the other projects covered in this book, this project explores the extra-European perspective through data gathered in an ethnographic research study at the Emergency Transit Mechanism

(ETM) of Niamey, the capital and largest city of Niger. Niger, belongs to the poorest and least developed countries in the world (UN, 2019). Like other countries of the Sahel, Niger is characterised by socio-economic problems caused by 'inherited colonial legacies (including the illogicality of many borders) and the transition from colonialism to undemocratic and often corrupt, militarised, neo-colonial regimes' (Bond, 2015, p. 346). Despite its relatively stable political situation, Niger faces violence, extremism and instability at its border (Cooke & Sanderson, 2016).

The United Nations High Commissioner for Refugees (UNHCR, 2020c) defines refugee sites as 'temporary facilities built to provide immediate protection and assistance to people who have been forced to flee due to conflict, violence or persecution'. Despite being considered a last resort (UNHCR, 2007), these settings have played and continue to play a crucial role in managing the 'refugee crisis' in Europe as well as in North Africa and Western Asia, where the roots of this 'crisis' are located. Sport programmes are largely used in refugee sites as a tool for social development (Ha & Lyras, 2013, p. 132; UNHCR et al., 2018). However, the abundance of sport sociological research on the topic of forced migration that has been carried out in recent years and commented on in the state-of-the-art of research has almost completely disregarded refugee sites (Waardenburg, Visschers, Deelen, & Liempt, 2018). To date, Sport for Development and Peace (SFDP) is the biggest programme that scientifically examines sport offers in this setting (Beutler, 2008; Ha & Lyras, 2013; Kidd, 2013). Despite the growing sociological and critical literature that has emerged on and within SFDP (Darnell, 2012; Giulianotti, 2011; Kidd, 2013), it remains an applied programme that assumes the utility of sport and focuses on implementing and improving it. Starting from a different perspective, this project aimed to broaden and question the current scientific discussion and intentionally avoided *a priori* assumptions on the beneficial effects of sport and evaluative aims.

In the late phase of the 'refugee crisis', Agadez, a city in central Niger, became a major route for refugees on their way to Europe. Its role became so important that UNHCR employees jokingly called the city 'the southernmost border of Lampedusa'. Despite being the poorest country in the region (or perhaps precisely for this reason), Niger agreed to host refugees in different ETMs,[6] which is a special form of refugee site.

Refugee sites are organisations that perform social work in the management of mass displacement (Malkki, 1995). 'Camp studies'

(D. Martin et al., 2020; Ramadan, 2013; Turner, 2016) assume that camps emerged as a spatial and bio-political means during the European colonial period to manage specific population groups or individuals. Camps are spaces of exception defined by (blurred) boundaries and (supposed) temporariness. They can be used to eradicate or save lives and for many other goals in between these two extremes (repression, violence, segregation, hospitality, care, solidarity). Importantly, social interactions in refugee sites are deeply influenced by the organisation's characteristic 'liminality' (Ager & Strang, 2008), which creates a limbic setting. The state of emergency and the scarcity of resources are important environmental factors for understanding the functioning of refugee sites. Finally, their operations are not only shaped by internal decision premises but also by structural couplings between sometimes contradictory logics and the direct involvement of many organisations.

The ETM of Niamey

> *aims to provide life-saving protection, assistance and long-term solutions to extremely vulnerable refugees trapped in detention in Libya, through temporary evacuation to Niger. The aim is to deliver protection and identify durable solutions, including resettlement for these refugees, who are predominantly Eritrean and Somalian. Their profiles mainly include survivors of torture or other forms of violence in the country of origin and/or transit countries (e.g. Libya) and others with compelling protection needs. Many of them are unaccompanied children and women and girls at risk.*
>
> (UNHCR, 2019)

The ETM includes three types of refugee sites in Niamey: the new and large site of Hamdallaye outside the city, the older and smaller Houses of Refugees, and the Health Centres in the city. Despite focusing on different specialisations, all sites provide their residents with water, food, medicine, shelter, and clothing. Beside securing livelihoods, they also provide psychological assistance, language classes and sport activities.

During the research period in May 2019, the Niger River, which crosses the city and mitigates its climate conditions, was semi-dry and the weather was very hot (between 35 and 45 degrees Celsius during the day, between 30 and 40 degrees Celsius at night). Islam is by far the dominant religion in Niger, and Ramadan was observed for almost the entire month. Although Ramadan is compatible with sport (Farooq & Parker, 2009; Roy et al., 2012), the scarce caloric intake and risk of dehydration due to the high temperatures certainly influenced the processes of the refugee sites (Afifi, 1997; Campante & Yanagizawa-Drott, 2015). However, the activities did not stop, including the sport activities. The analysis of the role of sport is based on ethnographic research of specific sport activities, including swimming, Taekwondo and football (Michelini, 2022).

In this setting, sport is assigned multiple and sometimes clashing meanings which rely mainly on the logic of sport 'performing/not performing' (Stichweh, 1990, p. 387), health 'health/illness' (Luhmann, 1983, pp. 169–170), and education 'teachable/unteachable' (Luhmann & Lenzen, 2002). While this is not an unusual phenomenon, the issues that characterise refugee sites, amplify and confuse the expectations of sport, turning it into a panacea.

03:54-Trainer 2: I am [name] and I am the [sport discipline] coach, we train them in sport in general, gymnastic, but specifically [sport discipline]. There is also my coach, I am his assistant, he is [name of the assistant coach]. We do not only teach [sport discipline]. Before starting, we try teaching them discipline, how to respect yourself, how to respect the others, how to be polite.

(Trainer 2, 2019)

Sport is carried out despite significant barriers connected to the scarcity of resources, the situation of emergency and the already mentioned environmental factors. In turn, this is a consequence of the diffused consideration of sport in all of the refugee sites' decision premises, at the programmatic, organisational, and personal levels (Luhmann, 2018). Finally, the health logic plays a crucial role for the legitimisation of organised sport activities at the ETM.

54:00-M: In the context of the lives of refugees, who have lost any regularity, sport can provide a new routine. They need routine and new rules. I hate to speak about having to give rules to refugees. But these rules are more a kind of 'life hygiene' which allow them to rebuild their lives and is the foundation for building and projecting them into the future. A real future, not only a dreamed up future.

(Manager 2, 2019)

Sport in refugee sites is visibly related to power that is a symbolically generalised communication medium, which enables acceptance of *alter*'s actions as premises and bonds for the actions of *ego* (Luhmann, 2017). Sport reinforces the unbalanced power relationship between refugees and the organisation's staff, entails disciplinary goals and is scrupulously promoted.

Despite the issues the context of refugee sites raise and the author's relatively sceptical attitude towards the SFDP (Giulianotti & Armstrong, 2013), the observations of the sport activities offered and the staff's accounts partly confirm the positive assumptions of sport activities in refugee sites.

> *01:13:01-M: I sometimes think that miracles do happen. I saw a man, Jay, when he came, he was very malnourished, shrunken, his belly was deflated, he was dirty, very dirty, tired and psychologically unstable. That was his condition. I saw him very often for a while. Then I didn't see him for three months, because I didn't visit the Health Centre. Then one day I saw a man with a big smile, he waved at me, it was National Refugee Day. I did not realise it was him, I could not recognise him. He was 10 kg heavier, just muscles. He was a changed man, a changed person. He had gotten into sport, Taekwondo, swimming, gym and he was very different, his life was different. His life was very different. You cannot take sport away from him, because it gave him a lot.*
>
> (Manager 2, 2019)

Yet, sport is not an 'island' where refugees merrily pass their time. Instead, sport entails major adaptations to the organisational specificity of the given refugee site. While retaining part of its meaning, pleasure and desires garnered on the field by both coaches and players (Rand, 2012; Thangaraj, 2015), sport absorbs and reproduces inherent contradictions of this specific context and its underlying goals (Agamben, 1998; Hartmann, 2016). In the limbic setting of refugee sites, sport becomes exceptional, multivalent, and relevant, but also elusive, ambiguous and coercive. For these reasons, basic sociological research can essentially contribute to a deeper and more complex understanding of sport in refugee sites.[7]

7.4 Forced migration and elite sport

The fourth project examined how critical life events, such as war, migration, and resettlement, influence and are influenced by socialisation in competitive sport. To answer the question 'How do forced migration and sport experiences influence the biographies of refugee athletes?', the sport careers of athletes with a refugee background were analysed. In addition to the leading perspectives of both sport and migration sociology, the biographical perspective also played a key role in this project. Biographical research formulates generalisations based on reconstructions of life histories (Fuchs-Heinritz, 2010). The mix of these three approaches sheds light on the relationships between individual lives, social structures, and historical processes through the accounts of sport biographies (ISA, 2020). According to Charles Wright Mills (2000, p. 143) 'social science deals with problems of biography, of history, and of their intersections within social structures'. While wars and migrations have influenced humans' (sport) biographies since the beginning of times (Bade, 2008; Manning & Trimmer, 2013), this fourth project identified distinguishing features and meanings of being an elite athlete with a forced migration background in the context of the 'refugee crisis'. Despite being guided by different questions and focusing exclusively on refugees, this project built and expanded on a research programme of athletes with a migration background carried out by Ulrike Burrmann's team at the TU Dortmund between 2010 and 2015 (Burrmann et al., 2017; Burrmann, Mutz, et al., 2015a; Zender, 2018).

In the course of life, individuals are more or less intensively included in and assume different roles within function systems. Research on talent reveals that critical life events can either advance or obstruct athletes' trajectories (John et al., 2019, p. 9). This assumption is confirmed by the biographies of successful refugee athletes such as Mohamed Farah (a Somali-born British long-distance runner, who won the 2012 and 2016 Olympic gold medals in both the 5,000 and 10,000 metre races) or Lopez Lomong (a South Sudanese-born US track and field athlete, who has won several national and international competitions). These cases demonstrate that the greatest sporting achievements are possible despite having a refugee background. Nevertheless, forced migration is a precarious event and is likely—at least in the short term—to cause psychological problems, weaken physical health and fitness and have a negative impact on the refugee's socio-economic status (Berry et al., 1987; Hobfoll et al., 1991; Yakushko et al., 2008). Finally, tragic stories about athletes who have disappeared or lost their lives during their forced migration exist as well. The prime example is that of former Olympic athlete Samia Yusuf Omar, who drowned close to the Italian coast during her forced migration.

She was trying to reach Europe to be able to continue her sport career (Krug, 2016). In 2016, the goalkeeper of The Gambia's national women's football team, Fatim Jawara, drowned in the Mediterranean trying to reach Europe (BBC, 2016a). Other professional Gambian football players have allegedly also lost their lives during their escape to Europe (Telegraph, 2016).

The analysis of this project in the context of Luhmann's systems theory has significant implications. From a constructivist perspective and following theoretical reflections of Koselleck (1979) on the time frames 'past, present and future', time is not only a subjective, but also a dynamic concept. In interviews with athletes, they re-construct 'pasts, presents and futures' by re-considering their sport careers and its development over time (Figure 7.3).

By considering athletes, this project examined the roles of individuals in relation to function systems. Neither individuals nor actions constitute social systems, but people are included on the basis of the specific roles they play in diverse social systems (Luhmann, 2005). Refugees risk becoming irrelevant in function systems and experience radical forms of exclusion (Luhmann, 1997), which has repercussions on their sport careers. Indeed, biographies are marked by life events. These can be critical or insignificant, unique or ordinary, fortunate or unfortunate. Some events are quickly forgotten while others leave indelible marks. The results of this project show that the influence of war-related events on sport careers is profound and reciprocal (Michelini, 2018). Unexpected results also emerged. For example, by playing for a club supported by the Syrian Army, the interviewees had a higher risk of being recruited by the Syrian Armed Forces.

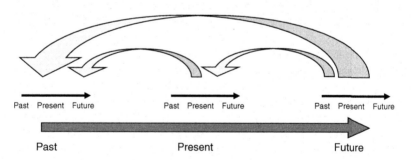

Figure 7.3 Dynamic understanding of time.

Lorans
10:22 L: It was just in Syria after 2011. It was also the last tournament for my club, we were the champions in the league. And then, because of the situation and the war there, we stopped training. (interrupted). [...]
10:39 Interviewer: For how long?
10:41 L: Like one and half years.
10:43 Interviewer: Okay. And you never trained?
10:46 L: No, that's why ... I'm going to say that. They asked us to fight because we are players, you know. When you're involved in sports, they want you to fight. (interrupted)

The resolve to engage in sport influenced important decisions before, during and after resettlement. In the examples below, sport was practiced despite the uncertain and dangerous situation, the position of water polo in the receiving country was considered in the choice of destination and the practice of sport became a reason for fatigue following migration.

Mufed
11:10 M: I trained until the very last days before leaving the country. Actually, 3 days before I got on that plane, I had a training session. But we made a sudden decision (interruption by third person). My family got the opportunity to migrate to Sweden, so we had to take it immediately within 3 or 4 days.

Lorans
2:42 L: Yes, and then water polo stopped in 2012 because of the war and there was no water polo anymore. That's also one of the reasons why I left Syria. So I left Syria in 2013 for Egypt.

Monzer (translation by the author)
0:53 M: [...]. At the beginning, I played in (name of a water polo club of a small German city). Two, two months. 2 and half months. But for me, it was very hard. Every day to (name of the small German city) [...] and back, yes. This is 3 hours or ... 3 and a half hours each day were lost. Yes, that is too much. I could not learn well. Work well.

As a critical life event, forced migration causes direct and indirect consequences, and had a severe impact on the sport careers examined; only one of the participants in the study was still engaged in elite sport. The possibility to pursue a professional career is technically still open for the other players as well, but is impracticable. Indeed, continuing to play water polo, even at an amateur level, requires significant sacrifices (Michelini, 2020-Submitted). Therefore, elite sport is considered impracticable in refugees' new daily routine (synchronic time), and missing trainings and having to compete at a crucial moment in their sport careers makes them now feel too 'old' (diachronic time).

> Monzer (translation by the author)
> *36:52 M: In the past, we were 16 years old, we were very, very, very good. We thought, I thought in the past, I wanted ... my dream (was) not to study, I dreamed about doing something with water polo, in the U.S. or in Europe. I thought in Europe I would have more opportunities, more opportunities to do something. Hmmm, but now I don't think the same way, because when you're 16, you can do so much. Now you have to be very good and very young in sport. [...] Yes, but this opportunity is already gone.*[8]

Consequently, the prioritisation of sport over other exigencies may facilitate but may also impede refugee athletes' successful inclusion in other contexts, for example, in education or economic systems. The results also show that the sample's high sport ambitions following resettlement changed and generally declined over the project's course of three years (Michelini, 2020a).

> Lorans
> *00:01:16 L: In the last two years my sport career ... I'm not playing water polo now at that really professional level. I'm also busy with studies. I actually left my old club [name of the club], where I was [playing when we last saw each other] in Sweden.*

The refugee athletes developed different strategies to cope with their sport ambitions within their new social context after resettlement: idealisation, which reinforces sport motivation through the attachment of external meanings; de-sportification, which strips competitiveness from sport; postponement, which delays the start of actively pursuing sport objectives; and abdication, which acknowledges and justifies the ceasing of a sport career.[9]

Notes

1 The section 'Articles by the author' of the bibliography entails the complete information on these articles.

Results of the Projects   67

2 Birte Krause, Kathrin Fahn (2019), and Jennifer Bruland contributed as student assistants to the creation of the category system and to the categorisation of the articles.
3 The annexes provide a more detailed description of these categories as well as anchor examples for each of them. In technical terminology, an anchor example is a clear and concise exemplification that works as an identifier of a category.
4 The arguments of this section can be deepened by reading three further essays of the author (see 'articles by the author': 1, 4, and 5 at the end of the book), which examine the communication of the catalogue of newspaper articles, conduct in-depth reviews of its contents and reflect on its function.
5 The 'additional resources' lists three articles (articles by the author: 2, 9, and 10) that empirically and theoretically deepen the results discussed above.
6 While humanitarian and moral reasons indubitably built up this decision, power and money may have also played a crucial role. Importantly, Niger is only a place of transit on the route of human traffickers and most of refugees have no intention to settle there.
7 The sixth entry of the list 'articles by the author' develops these arguments further.
8 Monzer was 22 years old at the time of the interview.
9 Three of the articles attached as annexes (articles by the author: 3, 7, and 11) further elaborate these results.

8 Overarching Discussion of the Results

Under an overarching theoretical model, this chapter considers the four projects previously described as an entire research programme on *forced migration and sport*. New knowledge will emerge by comparing and contrasting the individual projects. Concretely, sociological systems theory and its typology of systems introduced in the theory chapter was favoured over other theoretical models,[1] despite its lower dissemination. The extensiveness, complexity and requisite variety of its underlying theory (Luhmann, 1984b, p. 19; Willke, 2006, pp. 1–4) and the fact that systems theory was used in the majority of the projects under one theoretical framework make this model the most suitable candidate for an overarching consideration of the research.

To study the projects previously examined as a whole, the first step is to identify similarities and differences between the four projects against the backdrop of Luhmann's typology of systems.

Figure 8.1 illustrates this consideration and reveals particular similarities between two pairs of projects: both *Sport and Forced Migration in the Mass Media* and *Forced Migration and Elite Sport* examine society and the topic of elite sport. *Activities for Refugees in Sports Clubs* and *Physical Activity in Refugee Sites*, on the other hand, study sport offers provided for refugees in different organisational settings. The following section addresses these two pairs of projects as the first step of a progressive overarching consideration of this research by focusing on external and self-representations as well as on organisational logics.

8.1 Representations of refugee athletes

The two projects *Sport and Forced Migration in the Mass Media* and *Forced Migration and Elite Sport* applied completely different methods of data collection, but both considered elite athletes with a forced migration background. Comparing these two projects allows us to

DOI: 10.4324/9781003370673-8

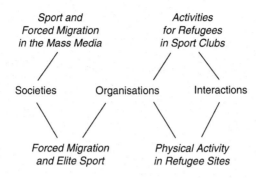

Figure 8.1 Research projects and types of systems.

contrast the athletes' perspectives and that of the mass media on the topic of forced migration and sport. This, in turn, allows detection of discrepancies and of the relationship between these two reconstructions of elite sport careers. The sometimes blurred difference between professional and non-professional athletes is determined by the function of sport in their lives, which is work-like for the professional, and hobby-like for the non-professional athlete. Despite this difference, which has important economic implications, both can be elite-level athletes or rather reach a level of competition at or close to a national standard (Delaney & Madigan, 2009, p. 94), and both can be hyper-included in sports (Bette & Gugutzer, 2012).[2] Importantly, the refugee athlete is a socially constructed role, which 'only exists insofar as he or she is named and recognized by others' (Hardy, 2003, p. 477). Because the code 'victory/defeat' lies at the core of any professional sport, the tendency to continuously refer to the athlete's past is superfluous, can be interpreted as a discriminatory practice, and creates role-specific expectations.

In interviews that appeared in newspapers and in those carried out by the author, the self-description of refugee athletes' inclusion in the sport system focuses on efforts and sacrifices made that lie beyond their successful sport careers. This book does not consider these declarations as factual representations of the truth, but instead as subjective reconstructions, which for different reasons may omit, modify, and embellish the individuals' lived experiences (Kühnle, 2020; Sparkes & Stewart, 2016). In these reconstructions, sport plays a relevant role in the biographies of refugee athletes before, during, and after their forced migration (Michelini, 2018). In the resettlement phase, sport assumed a different yet relevant role both among professional and non-professional elite athletes. The ambition but also the frustration of having missed the opportunity to turn sport into a job and a source of income is evident among most non-professional athletes interviewed. They often view the (sometimes) long forced breaks from training, the absence of support, and the lack of opportunities to demonstrate their actual value to be the main reasons for having been excluded from professional sport following their resettlement.

The mass media's external observation focuses on the celebration of successes, and the construction of sport heroes (and in rare cases antiheroes) against the backdrop of the 'refugee crisis' (Bette, 2019). Newspapers' reporting on refugee athletes is, for the most part, very positive and idealised (Michelini, 2021b). This suggests the influence of moral and political logic on that of both mass media and sport (Stichweh, 1990). Performance is nevertheless an important factor for retaining media sympathy and attention. The ups and downs involving Bakery Jatta (Michelini & Seiberth, 2022) and other refugee athletes (Agergaard, 2019; Burdsey, 2016) suggest that sympathy can quickly dissipate due to changes in public opinion or the athlete's alleged faults. In the German language, the word 'refugee' (*Flüchtling*) is appropriate in juridical terms, but has a negative connotation and is therefore avoided in 'politically correct' language (Duden, 2020). Nevertheless, refugee athletes are widely referred to as *Flüchtling* in the contents and headlines of each newspaper examined.

Interestingly, the findings of both projects reveal that the respective refugee athletes' sport careers are partly coupled to their relationships with the media. The project *Sport and Forced Migration in the Mass Media* indicates, amongst other results, that Yusra Mardini was able to secure her career as a professional swimmer through her successful relationship with the mass media (Michelini, 2021b). By contrast, the media's interest in Bakery Jatta was more a consequence of his successful career as a professional football player, and the scandal concerning his identity negatively affected his image and possibly also his performances (Michelini & Seiberth, 2022). The Syrian elite water polo players, who resettled in Europe and were the focus of the project *Forced Migration and Elite Sport*, had very little media visibility, and were proud and pleased to have received sporadic mention in the local news (for example in Noorden, 2014; Weckelman, 2018).

In these reports, they are mostly depicted as examples of 'good' refugees, namely those who have skills and have integrated in the receiving country. In this regard, the news articles are rather politicised and instrumental. The neoliberal discourse of hard work proclaims that anything is possible if you have the necessary perseverance. Social integration as well as a successful sport career is conflated in these

Overarching Discussion of the Results 71

representations and is turned into equal meritocracy fields, which allows social mobility and stratification. Refugee athletes are therefore represented as exceptional individuals, who are both model migrants and successful in sport. In turn, this reflects poorly on the majority of refugees, who are seen as not working as hard and as a burden on society.

Nevertheless, the refugee athletes' views when asked about this particular aspect were fairly positive because they had the chance of being in the spotlight of gaining visibility, and eventually establishing good connections in their sport and professional careers (Michelini, 2018).

8.2 Organisations and sport activities for refugees

To examine the sport activities provided to refugees by different organisations, both projects relied on ethnographic approaches for data collection, which included participant observations and interviews. Moreover, the projects focused on the perspective of sport staff involved in implementing these sport offers. The organisations and environments examined differ considerably: the first project examined sports clubs in Germany, one of the wealthiest countries in Europe (UN, 2019), where people voluntarily engage in activities with and for refugees. The second project considered refugee sites managed by UNHCR in Niger, an impoverished African country (UN, 2019), where contracted staff organise sport activities for the sites' residents. Though not surprising, the availability of sport activities for refugees in these organisations is not obvious in general. Indeed, sports clubs have no obligation to provide activities for special target groups, and the primary goal of refugee sites is to manage mass forced migration. The contingency that these activities would not have existed is therefore possible, while their availability and relevance implies the co-presence of factors that could influence these organisations' decisions. These decisions led to the creation of sport activities with similarities and differences, which are addressed below (Table 8.1).

Despite the completely different environments of the sports clubs and refugee sites considered, the research results (particularly in Michelini, 2022; Michelini et al., 2018) divulge numerous similarities. In both organisations, sport is believed to have properties that extend beyond the narrow sense of practising sport and include the promotion of health, education, discipline, and social integration. Nevertheless, most offers in both settings focused on competition and performance, and talented athletes were particularly welcomed and looked after. Moreover, the staff responsible for sport offers in both organisations

Table 8.1 Sport for refugees in sports clubs and refugee sites

Organisation Comparison	Sports club	Refugee site
Similarities	Multiple functions of sport (relevance of competition) Engaged trainers without a refugee background High fluctuation and mostly male participants	
Differences	National sport system Limited resources Volunteers Integrating participants	Liminal context Scarce resources Hired staff Recovering participants

were mostly locals without a migration background. They were highly motivated and engaged, had heterogeneous but solid sport expertise on average, and, despite the natural effects of work-related rationalisation, declared themselves devoted to the cause of helping people in need, in this case, the refugees. The activities offered in both settings were characterised by low and fluctuating participation. This problem resulted in instability, posed legitimisation problems, strained the general attitude towards the offers, and threatened their continued existence. In both settings, the participants were young to adult males. Female refugees only very rarely engaged in the sport activities offered. While signs of the participants' troubled pasts were sometimes discernible in their bodies and behaviours, the sport activities observed were relatively 'normal': extrapolated from their context, they were well-implemented and enjoyable activities which the participants could engage in with motivation and fun. Nevertheless, refugees in both organisations were mostly excluded from leading positions, while they would have been quite capable of administering their own sport activities amongst themselves or in a more participatory way (Harrell-Bond, 2002, p. 57).

There are differences between the two organisations' sport offers (particularly in Michelini, 2022; Michelini et al., 2018) in financial and human resources as well as the participants.

The refugee sites of Niamey struggled with very scarce resources for sport facilities and equipment while the sports clubs in Germany had comparatively abundant resources at their disposal. Nevertheless, German sport organisations reported that they had limited financial possibilities and, above all, faced problems recruiting and retaining volunteers to support activities for refugees.

Considering the organisation's human resources, while UNHCR contracted and paid staff to provide sport offers, German sports clubs relied on volunteers. This, in turn, implies different motivations for carrying out the activities and consequences for their cessation. The managers of sport offers in sport organisations were more intrinsically motivated but also more practical about the relevant issues and were prepared to give up the activities. By contrast, the managers of sport offers in refugee sites were extrinsically motivated and interested in the continuation of the offers.

Finally, differences between the participating refugees were observed as well. In Niger, the participants in sport offers were young to adult males who had mostly fled from Somalia, Eritrea, Nigeria, Burkina Faso, Mali, and South Sudan. The offers of German sports clubs, on the other hand, included mostly young to adult male Syrian participants. Their participants generally seemed to be in better physical and psychological shape. Obviously, this can be explained by the radical differences between the two settings and by the volatile but still safer situation in Europe.

As a form of social system, organisations allow for an efficient achievement of goals (W. R. Scott & Davis, 2015). Despite this crucial point and the high level of engagement of the individuals working for the organisations considered, it is evident that some organisational processes prevent better results in the work with refugees (Seiberth et al., 2013). Generally, the goal of sports clubs is not to integrate migrants, and the goal of refugee sites is not to carry out sport activities. Therefore, the resources allocated to this and other complementary aims are limited. By contrast, specific sport activities for refugees became a way for sports clubs and refugee sites to promote other goals as well as the overall self-maintenance of the organisation.

8.3 Holistic considerations of the research

To conclude the progressive overarching considerations of the research after separately reviewing the two pairs of comparable projects, the following section examines all four projects as one entire research programme.

Table 8.2 depicts how the four projects assessed different aspects of forced migration and sport. Comparing and contrasting the two pairs of projects sheds light on further results, which are discussed below in relation to the field of sport, the subjects, and the focus of the projects.

First, sport organisations apply strategies to exclude or include people with a forced migration and refugee background, both at the elite and at the amateur levels, which are overlapping yet distinct fields of sport in modernity (Stichweh, 2013, p. 93). The performance

74 Overarching Discussion of the Results

Table 8.2 Consideration of the four projects

Projects	*Sport and Forced Migration in the Mass Media* and *Forced Migration and Elite Sport*	*Activities for Refugees in Sports Clubs* and *Physical Activity in Refugee Sites*
Field of sport	Organised elite sport	Organised amateur sport
Subject	Athlete	Heads of sport offers
Focus	Individual biography	Organisation

principle guides elite sport, which is naturally closed to unqualified athletes and open to talented ones, irrespective of their migration background. This fundamental assumption does not at all preclude the phenomena of exclusion, discrimination, and racism (Hylton, 2005, 2010; Jarvie, 2005). With a few exceptions, the two research projects that focused on elite athletes with a refugee background revealed that they were in fact welcomed or that sports clubs actually vied for the best players. Some clubs actively advocated for 'their' refugee athletes, for example, by helping them resolve legal issues or by granting them financial assistance. It is impossible to establish the extent to which this generosity is connected to the objective of (cheaply) binding the athletes to the clubs or to other strategic goals. Despite this and the athletes' openly displayed gratitude, athlete-trainer issues emerged, especially in non-professional elite sport. The impossibility of the refugee athletes to train properly due to various issues (amongst others, related to their legal status, financial situation, and time scarcity) was a recurring reason for conflict. These reasons were sometimes understood and accepted or misinterpreted and rejected by trainers. The refugee status can generally intensify the naturally unbalanced power relationship between the coach and athlete (Cranmer & Goodboy, 2015). Amateur sport considers itself a social institution and perceives refugees as people in need of help. This attitude creates a qualitatively different but nonetheless unbalanced power relationship. Sometimes, the often-ascribed potentials of sport were perceivable in the sport offers organised for refugees. In the political and popular discourses, sport was seen as a way to promote refugees' health, education, discipline, and particularly their social integration (Council of Europe, 2020; European Commission, 2007; German Federal Government, 2007). While efforts to include refugees in amateur sport were sometimes naïve and simplistic, elements of a genuine welcome culture were observed in both German sports clubs and the refugee sites of Niamey.

However, the author also witnessed social conflicts, frustration, and the failure of these programmes. Interestingly, elite and amateur sports borrow and use the respective logics on certain occasions, for example, to legitimise, promote, and praise their own work with refugees.

Second, elite athletes and managers of amateur sport offers were highly motivated and willing to sacrifice their time and energy to engage in or organise sport activities. However, the real or perceived scarcity of resources and the instability of the context in general was a cause of distress for both elite athletes and managers of amateur clubs. A prolonged, unsatisfying, and wearisome engagement leads to frustration and even to dropouts or resignation from both these organisational roles. In the case of voluntary managers of sport activities, the fluctuating participation, and abandonment of sport participants, in particular, were the main reasons for disengagement in the work with refugees (Michelini & Burrmann, 2021). In the case of unpaid elite athletes, the prioritisation of other duties over sport was the main reason for dropping out (Michelini, 2018). This does not apply to professional and paid sport staff and athletes, whose inclusion in sport is work-related and a source of income (Michelini, 2021b, 2022). As sport professionals, they are dependent on the continuation of their sport activities or on their successful sport careers. Consequently, intrinsic motivation plays a less central role, and their main concern is the eventuality of losing their income from engagement in sport.

Third, the projects allowed for a comparison of the perspectives of individual biographies and sport organisations. A high attachment to sport is observable among elite athletes who experienced hardships before, during, and after their forced migration (Michelini, 2018). For some of the refugees who had not practised sport before or who had dropped out, forced migration was on occasion a factor that (again) brought them closer to sport. In the case of both a (new) beginning or continuation of sport, refugees mostly perceived their involvement in sport as being beneficial, but sometimes also as an obligation (Feuchter & Janetzko, 2018) or as very straining (Michelini, 2018). Turning the focus to sports clubs, the 'refugee crisis' was a social phenomenon that evidently had an impact on these organisations. Although the scientific community observed that sports clubs tend to reject innovation (Thiel & Meier, 2004, 2008), sport offers for refugees could be organised because typical blocking mechanisms against innovation were eliminated or bypassed (Michelini et al., 2018; Tuchel et al., 2021). Thereby, the tenacious initiatives of an individual or a small group of people among organisations' staff were the most relevant push factor. Moreover, the setting of clear goals and transparency for club members were also important factors to gain broad support within the club and in turn, for the organisation to successfully provide sport offers for refugees. Money played a relevant but not the primary role. Despite having only examined sports clubs that voluntarily opened up to refugees, blocking mechanisms were observed as well (Burrmann et al., 2019). These mostly emerged in the form of diffuse fears of losing the club's traditions. In most cases, however, the inclusion of refugees diminished contrasts, thus reviving the clubs' ideology and tradition. Social engagement with refugees seems to galvanise sports clubs and opens the door, especially of clubs with only a few members, to attracting new ones.

Notes

1 Models that consider interactions between the macro, meso, and micro societal levels are standard in sociological research. Together with numerous variations (Geels, 2002; Hajer, 2003), the 'boat' developed, amongst others, by Esser (1993), Coleman (1994), and Udehn (2002), is a classic multi-level model that is widely accepted in general sociology and in the sociology of sport (Breuer, Hoekman, Nagel, & van der Werff, 2015; Nagel, 2006, 2007; Nagel, Schlesinger, Bayle, & Giauque, 2015). This model's widespread acceptance and the fact that its main concepts are commonsensical outside the scientific community as well are major strengths. Luhmann (1987a) emphasises that systems theory rejects both the rationale and the nomenclature of the mainstream typology of social order.
2 For example, non-professional athletes can take their sport activity very seriously with the goal of becoming professional athletes.

9 Conclusion

Based on different questions, theories, methods, data, and approaches, this book examines various facets of the topic *forced migration and sport* in depth from a sociological perspective. The four projects analysed in the previous chapters reveal that:

- The press consistently covered the topic *forced migration and sport*, illustrating the newsworthiness of sport-related topics in the context of the 'refugee crisis'. The catalogue of article was embedded in previously existing debates on the 'refugee crisis' and the integrative power of sport. Also, in the case of sport, the construction of a critical situation served as a self-fulfilling prophecy and created feelings of uncertainty, discomfort, and fear.
- Sports clubs adapted to the 'refugee crisis', amongst others by providing specific sport activities for refugees. Previous experiences with integration constitute a solid foundation for further practices, and the implementation of sport offers for refugees is highly dependent on human resources. Sports clubs exhibited an unexpected dynamism and high capacity to mobilise resources.
- Refugee sites have high expectations of sport and organise it notwithstanding the existent obstacles. Despite the impact of this setting on social interactions, sport retains part of its meaning, joy, pleasure, and desires that are generally associated with engagement in sport. Yet this liberation only exists within the boundaries of sport activities. Therefore, sport is only seemingly a sanctuary where opportunities for recreation are being offered to refugees. At the refugee sites, sport becomes something extraordinary and multivalent, but also elusive and ambiguous.
- The refugee athlete is a socially constructed role that generates both positive and negative implications and contradictions. Forced migration is a critical life event that constitutes an impediment to

DOI: 10.4324/9781003370673-9

a sport career at many levels. However, the sport biographies of elite athletes with a refugee background are fairly heterogeneous. While sport is of a high relevance after resettlement, most athletes dropped out or reduced their involvement in sport.

Based on this information and its interconnections, the leading question of this book 'What role does sport play in the context of the "refugee crisis"?' can be 'answered' as follows: over time, sport assumed different roles during the 'refugee crisis'; this event and the sport system profoundly and reciprocally influenced each other; this relationship echoes and reproduces broader social phenomena of inclusion and exclusion, which are deeply entangled with power. Sport mirrored both feelings of intense solidarity and animosity, which alternated and coexisted throughout the 'refugee crisis'. The overall adaptation of the sport system was dynamic and positive. However, many of the actions were naive, superficial, strategic, selective, and racialised. The role and potential of sport were widely overestimated and romanticised both in external and self-representations as well as in the organisations considered here. This could have positive implications because this over-optimism might foster action and ambition. Nevertheless, the existing but relatively scarce potential of sport should be utilised and optimised instead of exaggerated and (self-)celebrated. To further specify and manifest this statement, the next section provides a sociological analysis (see: Luhmann, 1997, pp. 36–41), which focuses on the role of sport in Europe in general and during delimited periods of the 'refugee crisis'. Next, a reflection on the limitations of this investigation and future perspectives of research on this social phenomenon are discussed.

9.1 The role of sport within the 'refugee crisis'

After radically reducing the complexity of the topic at hand to formulate an answer to the leading research question, this section reconstructs part of the complexity by elaborating this answer in specific fields of sport. This analysis is based on the projects discussed above, on the current state of research and on the broader expertise the author has developed on this topic over his six years of scientific work. The role of sport in the context of the 'refugee crisis' is discussed by considering three phases (2013–2014, 2015–2016, and 2017–2018), three fields of sport (elite, amateur, and leisure), and Europe as a specific setting (Figure 9.1).[1]

Conclusion 79

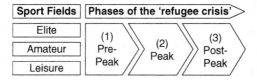

Figure 9.1 Fields of sport and phases of the 'refugee crisis'.

This analytical strategy allows for an examination of relevant selected facets of this broader social phenomenon. These categories partly overlap, may have been conceived differently, and only have explanatory power under a specific understanding, which will be further explicated below.

9.1.1 Elite sport

The role of elite sport is considered with regard to its capacity to include refugee athletes in the three phases of 'the refugee crisis':

1 The pre-peak phase of the 'refugee crisis' only very marginally touched on the sport system at the elite level. As talented athletes are valued in elite sport, clubs were eager to secure new talents, even though they could not debut immediately for local clubs due to bureaucratic regulations. Sport disciplines such as football, combat sports, and athletics, in particular, benefitted sporadically but quickly from the arrival of new talented athletes on European soil.
2 During the peak phase of the 'refugee crisis', sport talents were also among the mass of forcibly displaced persons. The first refugee athletes that migrated during the 'refugee crisis' were able to integrate as professionals in the European elite sport system. For example, football clubs included refugees at the highest competition levels, such as in the cases of Bakery Jatta in Germany, Musa Juwara in Italy, and Jacob Viera in the UK (Stone, 2018). Moreover, the IOC created a Refugee Olympic Team (ROT) in 2015, which competed in front of a huge audience at the 2016 Summer Olympics in Rio de Janeiro, Brazil (Abd Rahim, Diah, & Aman, 2018).
3 In the post-peak phase of the 'crisis', processes of routinisation and stabilisation were observable in the field of elite sport. A few successful refugee athletes became national or international celebrities. Contrary to the previous phases, critical voices grew louder and scandals involving refugee athletes emerged, such as in the case of Bakery Jatta (Michelini & Seiberth, 2022).

80 Conclusion

Elite sport was generally expected to be highly inclusive of refugee athletes but only slightly adapted its routine and rules for facilitating their inclusion. As a form of organised and competitive sport practised within the scope of official sports clubs, federations, and events, the inclusion of specific population groups is neither desired nor possible. Indeed, inclusion in elite sport is strictly connected to performance and measured through rankings of athletes, qualifying standards, and contests. As previously stated, forced migration implies a radical change in an individual's life and potential psycho-social problems, which are significant impediments to sport performance. The self-description and social perception of elite sport is that of an open, inclusive, and fair arena, but refugee athletes are penalised due to the exclusive orientation towards competition, because their forced migration in most cases implies major impediments to their sport activity. Paraphrasing Aristoteles (350 BCE/1932), the sport system attempts to make unequal things equal. While fairy tales of refugee athletes in sport are possible and are powerful symbols of redemption, changing a system that generates radical inequality is more important than echoing the rare success cases. Instead, the few adaptations of the sport system at the elite level were rather symbolic or functional in terms of its performance-oriented logic and not of a humanitarian nature (Hoberman, 2011, p. 17).

This, notwithstanding, elite sport also represented an important anchor for some of the refugees who had a sport background and also had a significant economic impact on some professional athletes. Importantly, sport represents employment for professional athletes, and the breakdown of the sport system in their countries of origin resulted in the cessation of their profession and income. Similarly, the impossibility of non-professional elite athletes to also engage in sport was a reason for leaving their countries of origin (Michelini, 2018). Finally, professional athletes also decided to leave their countries during this period, using the opened refugee routes to seek a better future elsewhere, despite having a secure job in sport. For example, half of the first team players of Banjul United, a professional Gambian football team, left their home in 2016, hoping to be accepted as refugees in Europe (BBC, 2016a; Palliggiano, 2016; Telegraph, 2016). Moreover, six track and field athletes of the Refugee Olympic Team deflected after competing abroad (Cullum, 2021; Heim, 2018; Streule, 2020). Against the backdrop of the asylum-migration nexus (Gutiérrez Rodríguez, 2018; Stewart, 2008),[2] the acceptance or rejection of refugee status may ignore the actual cause for migration. Newly arrived refugee athletes had to adjust to their new situation, endure the

Conclusion 81

bureaucratic process of refugee assessment, and re-join the sport system. While this re-inclusion can theoretically take a long time, most narratives of refugee athletes indicate that finding a new club was amongst the first aims they pursued after their resettlement (Michelini, 2018). This is logical as sport is highly relevant for elite athletes and plays an important role in the (re-)creation of continuity and meaning following forced migration. Instead, finding the 'right club' and achieving past performances again is a longer and more difficult process, depicted as quite compelling given the barriers refugees face immediately following resettlement and without contacts in the local sport scene.

9.1.2 Amateur sport

The role of amateur sport in the 'refugee crisis' is examined here through the alleged integrative function of sports clubs:

1   The few refugees that arrived during the early phase of the 'crisis' represented a relevant but not overwhelming impulse for European sports clubs. During the 'refugee crisis', grassroots sport was expected to help refugees integrate into their new homeland. However, these organisations responded differently to the occurring events, adopting varying degrees of openness or closedness, often taking a wait-and-see approach (Tuchel et al., 2021). During this phase, sports clubs initiated adaptation processes centred around the inclusion of and binding the newly arriving refugees. Those with previous experiences in the area of integration could build upon and elaborate their already established organisational culture.
2   Several changes were observed within sports clubs during the peak phase of the 'refugee crisis'. Aiming to adapt to this crisis and to include refugees, the scarcity of knowledge, resources, and time forced sports clubs to rely on the basic operations that were known, possible, and intrinsic to the organisations (Stichweh, 2018). Using these operations to include refugees presupposes innovation readiness or the existence of a sociocultural memory of previous similar experiences. Therefore, sports clubs that included refugees or committed to taking them in often perceived this phase as intense, invigorating, and overwhelming (Burrmann et al., 2019). The elusive and loaded expectations were partly unrealistic and limited by sports clubs' possibilities. Sport entailed different goals, often with the intention of integrating refugees. It was an

arena where the welcome culture (Heinrich-Böll-Stiftung, 2016) was sometimes displayed and applied in practice at the local level (Burrmann, 2020). Sport organisations became a setting of engagement for refugees in different ways: sport facilities were utilised as emergency shelters for newly arriving refugees; specific sport activities (mostly free of charge) were offered; sport organisations were used as a platform to distribute clothes donations. Sport organisations were thereby sometimes able to influence (in the best case, in a positive way) the lives of refugee participants. With the negative change in public attitude towards refugees in 2016 (Georgiou & Zaborowski, 2017), the resources and possibilities of sports clubs to support refugees also weakened.

3 In the late phase of the 'refugee crisis', sport organisations adapted to the crisis based on their previous experiences about what had worked and what had not, abandoned or modified non-functional practices and routinised and improved functional ones. Within these organisations' programmes, special refugee sport offers were often shelved and integrated into the club's 'normal' activities (Michelini & Burrmann, 2021). Sometimes, refugees left sports clubs because they faced new exigencies, found other activities to engage in, or were displaced or repatriated (Michelini, 2018). For this and other reasons, much of the sports clubs' initial energy and enthusiasm diminished and some of their staff *a posteriori* view the preceding years with disillusionment or even disappointment (Michelini & Burrmann, 2021). This does not mean that the previous status quo was restored. Instead, the experiences collected during the refugee crisis purportedly inspired the culture and decision premises of sports clubs. Amateur sport evolved in the wake of the 'refugee crisis' and in all probability remains more prepared to include migrants or new waves of refugees in the future.

Sports clubs are diffusely distributed in most European countries and are the backbone of the field of sport (Breuer et al., 2015). Notwithstanding ongoing discussions about their actual role in integration (Dowling, 2020; Seiberth & Thiel, 2010; Seiberth et al., 2013), sports clubs have an inclusive history of migrants (S. Braun & Nobis, 2011; Nagel et al., 2020). Therefore, as in the context of previous migration crises, sports clubs were expected to be an important engine for the integration of refugees in Europe (Council of Europe, 2020; ENGSO, 2020; UNHCR, 2020b). The data analysed indicate the existence of an eradicated 'savage imaginary' (Hesse & Sayyid, 2006) about refugees' sport skills upon their arrival, which are stereotypically considered row and low. However, most of the refugees that arrived in Europe had a basic sport background and a 'normal' dispersion of talent. Whether they decided to engage in sport after their resettlement depended on many factors. However, many of them were exposed—at least for a short period of time—to a bureaucratic process, which notably impeded their freedom and activity in many fields and they thus had more free time than usual. This time was sometimes occupied with sport, which was frequently accessible to them (Breuer, 2017). For some refugees, sport (clubs) became an important place of socialisation, others left them, sometimes after a comparatively long and intensive time, and others never found their way back into sport.

9.1.3 Leisure sport

The role of leisure sport during the 'refugee crisis' was examined in the setting of European emergency reception centres, which are refugee sites that differ from those constructed for other aims and in other continents:

1 In Europe, the need to manage mass displacement reached an emergency level in the initial phase of the 'migration crisis', which triggered the installation of refugee sites. The development of spontaneous camps into regular refugee sites is a prototypical development. Temporary shelters created by refugees along their route, close to a country border or at other assembly points, evolved into fixed camps through the intervention of intergovernmental organisations, states, and ONGs (Doidge & Sandri, 2019; Sandri, 2018). As is the case in other sites around the world, mostly children and youth engaged in spontaneous play and informal sport in such settings in Europe (Beutler, 2008; Huizinga, 1939/2004). The newer, poorer, and more provisional the sites are, the less structured and limited the possibilities to engage in sport (Paardekooper, De Jong, & Hermanns, 1999).
2 Managing the peak of the 'refugee crisis' in Europe consisted in part of developing different emergency solutions to shelter refugees (Hunger & Kersting, 2019). Existing and newly built refugee sites hosted an increasing number of refugees. These places included initial reception centres and provisional shelter solutions, which were often arranged in sport halls. The momentary requisition and conversion of sport facilities into refugee sites posed a notable disruption for the sport system. Sport was also an important activity in European refugee sites, just like elsewhere, to

84 Conclusion

pass time, stay fit, and have fun (Lewek & Naber, 2017). The coercive and palliative function of sport in refugee sites were the other face of the coin (Michelini, 2022). Moreover, special collaborations between reception centres and sports clubs were often quickly arranged to implement sport offers within or outside the refugee sites (Burrmann et al., 2019).

3 Despite important exceptions such as Lampedusa, Calais, and Lesbos, many emergency structures installed to deal with the 'refugee crisis' in Europe have been reduced, merged, reconverted, or dismantled. With their disappearance, the collaboration experiences between sports clubs and refugee sites have also ceased. Without this connection, sports activities were terminated or normalised as regular offers of sports clubs. The reduction of refugee sites on European soil does not imply a return to the pre-'crisis' order, but instead indicates a temporary control of migration movements to Europe (D. Martin et al., 2020). Despite this, the causes of the 'crisis' remain largely unresolved and refugee sites in other regions are still dealing with alarming phenomena such as instability and overcrowding.

During the 'refugee crisis', refugee sites consolidated their key role in the modern management of mass migration (D. Martin et al., 2020). Moreover, while refugee sites have mainly been constructed outside Europe in recent decades, often to stop incoming migration flows, refugee sites managed to 'arrive' in Europe during the 'refugee crisis'. Agamben (1998) describes refugees confined in reception sites as '*homo sacer*', or persons who are outside the law or beyond it. In this setting, they live a 'bare life', which 'is included in the juridical order solely in the form of its exclusion' (Agamben, 1998, p. 12). For these reasons, the sites' contradictory existence and the vulnerability of their inhabitants are considered nomos of our time (Agamben, 1998). Despite being an extremely heterogeneous group (Malkki, 1995), the operations at refugee sites generate 'doing refugee' processes (Schütte, 2019; West & Zimmerman, 1987),[3] which are visible in the examined sport activities as well. At the same time, refugees have agency and are not 'apolitical, docile, dependent recipients who benefit enormously from humanitarian intervention' (Besteman, 2016, p. 29). Some sociological studies suggest that the 'dependency syndrome' affects the residents of these sites (Abdi, 2005; Boesen, 1985). However, this has been considered an imaginary of the dominant class (Reid & Al Khalil, 2013). The prolongation of residency in such sites is often frustrating and implies high availability of time, which is sometimes occupied with sport.

9.2 Limitations

This book does not exhaustively contemplate the topic at hand. Instead, there are further relevant settings (i.e. schools and playgrounds) and variables (i.e. religion and gender) that have not been considered. The inclusion of other settings in the realms of organised and particularly of informal sport would broaden and complement the examination of this multifaceted phenomenon. Additionally, including further case studies from outside Germany and Europe would reinforce the description of the 'refugee crisis' as a worldwide issue and would meet the international ambitions of this research. It must be stressed, however, that a research programme can always be expanded but it is also limited in resources and undergoes a process of saturation, which diminishes the added value of additive research. Moreover, as the 'refugee crisis' is a transnational (Agergaard, 2018) phenomenon, part of the research carried out in this book exceeds the national borders within which it was carried out.

Examining the intersections (Collins & Bilge, 2020) that emerge from having a refugee background and other systems of inequality is likely to generate a better understanding about the topic at hand. Collins and Bilge (2020, p. 14) define 'intersectionality' as the investigation of 'how intersecting power relations influence social relations across diverse societies as well as individual experiences in everyday life'. While the focus of the projects lied on the implications of forced migration, considering other categories such as race, class, gender, sexuality, religion, nation, ability, ethnicity, and age as being interrelated and mutually influence one another has the potential of creating knowledge about specific forms of discrimination and their unique dynamics and effects. This said, incorporating additional complex levels of analysis to this already intricate research might also have limited the generation of results and their significance.

Further issues have influenced the research carried out. Despite the important implications of a radical constructivist position (Fox, 2001; Phillips, 1995; Von Glasersfeld, 1995), meta-theoretical questions related to ontology and epistemology will be ignored in this section. Nevertheless and importantly, systems theory considers researchers to be second-order observers, who, through selected distinctions, can shed light on the blind spots of other observations but not on their own ones (Luhmann, 1997). That having been said, this section self-critically reflects on the general issues related to the methodological and practical limitations of this research.

9.2.1 Methodological aspects

Regardless of the strengths and weaknesses of the methods applied in the individual projects, three main overarching methodological issues influenced this research.

First, all four projects relied on qualitative and interpretative methods (Lloyd, 2000) and analysed data collected through documents, interviews, participant observations, and fieldwork. The methodology chapter considers the limitations of these individual methods. According to Bradley (1993), four main factors influence qualitative research in general: (1) the researcher's (subjective) interpretation; (2) the pre-defining effects of the design of the research; (3) the impossibility of understanding the experiences of others; and (4) the intrinsic problem of trustworthiness. However, quantitative research also has inherent limitations (Ochieng, 2009), and using qualitative methods is thus not a weakness *per se*. Importantly, there was sometimes no alternative to the approaches implemented, as further argued below. Nevertheless, the use of questionnaires or other quantitative instruments would have been a way to diversify the empirical data and open the possibility to apply a mixed-methods design (Creswell & Creswell, 2017).

A second limitation of the research underlying the habilitation is the consideration of refugees' perspectives, which is the focus of only one of the four projects. Giving refugees a voice is a challenging, ethically loaded, romanticised, and sometimes unreachable goal within refugee studies (Ghorashi, 2008; Pittaway, Bartolomei, & Hugman, 2010; Sukarieh & Tannock, 2013). Researchers who aim to capture the voices of refugees must reflect on the main reasons why this could be difficult (Pittaway et al., 2010). As a vulnerable group, refugees may avoid answering certain questions (Hartley et al., 2017, p. 1192), particularly if they are in the process of migrating, have newly migrated, have a complicated juridical position or risk being repatriated. Moreover, being asked deeply personal questions may be a source of stress and may even re-traumatise the refugee or remind the refugee of his or her status determination process (C. Hardy, 2003). For these and other reasons, directly accessing refugees as a source of information is possible and ethically sustainable only after establishing direct contact with them based on trust and friendship. Sport has been part of the project's setting, in which such relationships evolved. Finally, Spaaij et al. (2019) note that research on *forced migration and sport* would profit from a decolonisation process. Most scientific work on this topic has to date been carried out by European researchers, who align themselves 'with the policy priority of sport as a means for promoting the integration' (Spaaij et al., 2019, p. 14). Agreeing with the critical discourse on integration in/through sport (Schinkel, 2018), this book voluntarily shifts attention to other topics. Moreover, part of this research focused on the struggles of refugees and was documented based on their own words and developed with their cooperation. Nevertheless, this research, as well as all 'official' scientific work performed on this topic to date, far from genuinely applies the proposals of the decolonisation movement to research (Land, 2015; Smith Tuhiwai, 1999; Tuck & Yang, 2012). While some of these suggestions are rooted in the indigenous rights movement and cannot be fully applied to displaced persons, the implementation of practices such as supporting refugee agendas, understanding different perspectives, and applying principles of cultural protocols, ethics, co-design, and the dissemination of findings are possible. In the author's opinion, involving refugees in research on forced migration may be the key to decolonising this topic.

Third, the author played a central role in the data collection process and analysis. Despite careful methodological reflection and interaction with colleagues, his belief system may have influenced the research process. From an epistemological standpoint, the understanding (Gadamer, 1960/2004), or rather the scientific knowledge developed within a work process, needs to be considered against the researcher's social and personal contexts as well. The 'refugee crisis' was a contemporary and heated topic when this research was carried out and the author approached it with a pre-understanding (Gadamer, 1960/2004). This indicates an intentional structure of feelings and thoughts, which includes emotions, knowledge, political views, training, and experience (Nyström & Dahlberg, 2001; Whannel, 2013). The hermeneutic circle (Packer & Addison, 1989) refers not only to the co-development of understanding and pre-understanding, but also to the awareness of their interaction and its effect on understanding. As this process is subjective and potentially boundless, some of the insights of this research may reflect a present but transitory state of this hermeneutic circle.

9.2.2 Practical aspects

The research presented in this book was mostly carried out without or with very little funding. Despite having applied for numerous grants and funds, the external financing raised was insufficient to conduct the four projects presented above to their fullest potential. Moreover, certain external obstacles and importantly the COVID-19 pandemic hampered the further development of parts of the projects. Further research-related meetings of the project *Forced Migration and Elite Sport* were cancelled. The Syrian water polo team should have officially participated in a water polo tournament for the first time since the outbreak of the civil war, which was scheduled for March 2020 at the FINA Games in Tunis. In the context of the project *Physical Activity in Refugee Sites*, a second ethnographic study was planned at the refugee sites of Niamey in August 2020. The pandemic and the escalating violence in the Sahel zone suspended this follow-up. Similar reasons prevented research at other refugee sites.

Other impediments were of a legal nature. As a post-doc conducting research on a migration-related topic at an international university, it is evident that the author's work may have implied travelling. However, more than one trip to the so-called G-35-Area (which mainly coincide with Africa, South America, Australia, and South Asia) were denied due to TU Dortmund's current restrictive regulations on work-related travel. That is, authorising university employees to travel to this extended Southern Hemisphere is expensive and extremely problematic for the heads of faculties with regard to legal and insurance-related aspects.

Besides feelings of frustration of being deterred in carrying out research activities, the universities' dilemma is understandable. On the one hand, they have to protect themselves and their workers. On the other, they have to stage themselves as international players of the global academic arena. Indubitably, the tragic murder of Giulio Regeni in 2016 during his PhD research in Cairo (Pyper, 2016) is something that should never have happened nor should it ever happen again. Nonetheless, while respecting security standards, on-site research on current and relevant social phenomena should be encouraged and not hampered by outdated organisational guidelines.

9.3 Future perspectives

Starting from the critical reflection presented above, this book concludes with the identification of research gaps, the formulation of a future scientific agenda, and, finally, an appeal to the scientific community.

9.3.1 Research gaps

Considering the work carried out within the context of the broader state of research on the topic *forced migration and sport*, three main research gaps emerged.

First, international and cooperative projects are rare and lack a sociological perspective. The research landscape is fragmented in a multitude of small-scale studies. While this fragmentation has the advantage of creating a variegated and independent picture of different facets of the topic, broad and coordinated efforts would generate an optimisation of the research processes, particularly the comparative potential, which is not fully reachable by contrasting the results of the individual projects a posteriori. For this reason, the development of broader and more ambitious research projects is warmly encouraged.

Second, future research should be decolonised and carried out by or in cooperation with scientific staff with a refugee background. In the short term, refugees should be involved in the ongoing research processes, not only as data sources but also to provide their analysis and interpretation as co-researchers. In the medium term, refugees themselves should lead and carry out research on forced migration. Obviously, a refugee background often implies a situation of socioeconomic inequality, which constitutes a barrier to an academic career (Potter & Roksa, 2013). For this reason, their involvement in academic research is unlikely to occur spontaneously. Instead, it would require the creation of solid support programmes to restore equity and possibilities for refugees to use education as a pathway towards social mobility. Moreover, this requires systemic and personal initiatives within the university system to foster talented students with a refugee background in pursuing higher academic qualifications. Despite many obstacles, hiring researchers with a refugee background to carry out scientific work on the phenomenon of forced migration would be a fruitful way to decolonise research in this area.

Third, existing systematic review analyses (Michelini, 2020b; Middleton et al., 2020; Spaaij et al., 2019) highlight that existing research focuses on only few selected topics, namely that of health promotion, integration and social inclusion, and barriers and facilitators to participation in sport and physical activity. One of the strengths of this book is that it considers additional topics such as refugee sites and refugee athletes. A further broadening of the foci would diversify and deepen the status of research. Moreover, a selection bias intrinsically affects research on *forced migration and sport*, because the main methods of data collection and the recruitment of participants is conducted by sport organisations and involve refugees who are active in sport. By contrast, information on refugees who are not active in sport or who have dropped out is almost completely lacking. Nevertheless, it would be important to enrich the scientific discourse on inequality in sport by exploring exclusion mechanisms specific to refugees. As regards the present research programme, particularly the potential of parts of the projects, was not fully realised. Amongst other topics, the following section explains ways to develop these further.

9.3.2 Future scientific agenda

Suggestions for future research have been included in the literature analysis chapter and emerge from the gaps discussed above. This section proposes further concrete developments of the projects *Physical Activity in Refugee Sites* and *Forced Migration and Elite Sport*.

The research carried out for the project *Physical Activity in Refugee Sites* is particularly relevant because these settings have played and continue to play a crucial role for managing the 'refugee crisis' in Europe as well as in other continents that generate or receive masses of forcefully displaced persons. Moreover, sport programmes are often used as a tool for social development in refugee sites (Ha & Lyras, 2013, p. 132). As discussed in the state of research chapter, Sport for Development and Peace is a well-developed scientific programme for sport in refugee sites, but is of an applied nature (Beutler, 2008; Darnell, 2012; Giulianotti, 2011; Ha & Lyras, 2013; Kidd, 2013). By describing and analysing sport activities in refugee sites without evaluative or educative purposes, the project *Physical Activity in Refugee Sites* explores a mostly ignored topic under sociological aspects (Waardenburg et al., 2018).

When this book was written, the author's scientific work (Michelini, 2018, 2020a, 2020-Submitted) was the only academic research that focused on elite-level athletes with a refugee background, whose selected stories were anecdotally reported by the media or contained in autobiographies (Farah, 2013; Lomong & Tabb, 2012; Mardini, 2018). The research carried out within the scope of the project *Forced Migration and Elite Sport* sheds light on some psychosocial phenomena that need to be further considered by including additional groups of elite and super-elite refugee athletes and sport disciplines (L. Hardy et al., 2017). Besides contrasting migrant groups, further research would ideally also compare refugees' career paths in other fields beyond sport, for example in music, art, and other fields (Dany, Mallon, & Arthur, 2003; John et al., 2019). As time plays a crucial role in this regard, longitudinal studies could generate additional information by following the developments of refugee athletes' sport careers over a longer period.

9.3.3 Call to the scientific community

This book ends with an appeal to the scientific community, in general, and to sport sociologists, in particular, to contribute to the continuation of the intensive and productive work on the topic *forced migration and sport* that has been carried out in recent years. The motivation underlying this call is the recent occurrences, which despite seemingly unrelated to the 'refugee crisis' at first glance may influence its future development and legacy.

First, social inequality is (still) prevalent and rife (Evans et al., 2020). The so-called George Floyd protests[4] in 2020 were a catalyst for worldwide protests, resistance, and activism. The 'Black Lives Matter' (BLM) anti-racism movement, in particular, has given rise to discussions and debates on economic and health inequalities, freedom and politics, and 'has given new impetus to moral panics surrounding migration and what is often been described as the "migrant crisis" in Europe and North America' (Evans et al., 2020, p. 289). Refugees, particularly those in the process of migrating, living illegally in a foreign country, trapped between borders, imprisoned in detention centres or residing in refugee sites are very vulnerable to discrimination, harassment, and violence (Freedman, 2016). While this fact is widely documented by the media and independent agencies, it is highly plausible that this reporting points to the visible peak of a huge, submerged iceberg. Following resettlement and the legalisation of their status, refugees face substantially more discrimination than other migrant groups (Çelebi, Verkuyten, & Bagci, 2017).

Second, the 'refugee crisis' was a leading popular, political, and scientific issue between 2015 and 2018, which has frequently been discussed in relation to sport (Evans, Blackwell, et al., 2020; Michelini, Bortoletto, & Porrovecchio, 2021; Nauright, Zipp, & Kim, 2020). At the beginning of 2020, the outbreak of the COVID-19 pandemic magnetised societal attention and 'miraculously' concluded (the social perception of) the 'refugee crisis' (Bortoletto et al., 2021). Obviously, the 'migration crisis' did not simply disappear with the outbreak of the coronavirus. Current developments related or unrelated to the 'coronavirus crisis' suggest that the phenomenon of forced migration will continue to play an important societal role. Indeed, limitations to movement considered necessary to manage the virus make it difficult for migrants and asylum seekers to access protection, and may further exacerbate inequality, discrimination, and exploitation (Chugh, 2020).[5] Moreover, it has already been acknowledged that sport could play a special role for displaced communities during the pandemic (UNHCR, 2020a).

92 Conclusion

For these reasons and with the hope that scientific work may resonate on policymaking and opinion-formation processes (Black, 2001; Holmes & Castañeda, 2016), it is important for the sport sociological community to continue to contribute through its work to keep the attention high on the dramatic situation of refugees all over the world. Many critical analyses of the 'refugee crisis' mentioned in this text invoke social responsibility. As Foucault (1990) and other critical sociologists (Escobar, 1984) mused over other topics, this book stresses the importance of solving the contradictions embedded in the modern political order, which produces refugees (Agamben, 1998). A transformation of the refugee system is urgently needed (Betts, 2013, 2011; Betts & Collier, 2017). Specific to the field of sport, many good and bad practices have been identified in this research. This, notwithstanding, the dark side of sport is concealed in the mass media, social and political discourses. Often, the consideration of sport as a social panacea is built upon a 'magical thinking' (Hoberman, 2011, p. 18), which needs to be further deconstructed. The sport sociological community can contribute to creating a more honest and objective consideration of sport's role in the context of refugee help. Paraphrasing a widely cited quotation of Foucault in a debate with Chomsky (1971): 'The real task of sport sociology is to criticize the apparently neutral and independent role of sport in such a manner that the political violence obscurely exercised through it will be unmasked' (Michelini, 2021a, p. 276).

Notes

1 The following section builds on the theoretical explanation of the mechanisms beyond social change, crisis, time, the sport system, and space contained in the chapter on the theoretical framework.
2 See the definition of the main terms.
3 'Doing gender' is a term coined by West and Zimmerman (West & Zimmerman, 1987) in their homonymous article. It indicates the idea that gender is not an innate quality of individuals and instead is 'a routine, methodical, and recurring accomplishment' (West & Zimmerman, 1987, p. 126). Similarly, 'refugee' is a label that creates expectations and obligations, which constitute a rigid accountability structure. On this basis, refugees are judged and judge themselves in terms of 'good/bad', 'successful/unsuccessful', 'included/excluded'.
4 This series of protests and unrest against brutality and racism in policing began in the United States in Minneapolis in response to the death of George Floyd, after police officer Derek Chauvin knelt on Floyd's neck for over nine minutes during his arrest on 26 May 2020 (Barbot, 2020).
5 At the same time, 'fake news' about a lack of workforce in Europe caused by the pandemic has created new migration movements from Africa (Economist, 2020).

Articles by the Author*

1. Michelini, E., & Seiberth, K. (2022). Refugee, Footballer and (Anti-)Hero: The Case of Bakery Jatta. A Discourse Analysis of German Newspapers. *Soccer and Society*, Online first. doi:10.1080/14660970.2022.2080668
2. Michelini, E., & Burrmann, U. (2021). A Preliminary Impact Model for the Integration of Young Refugees through Sport Programmes. *CuSSoc*, 6(2), 265–281.
3. Michelini, E. (2020-Submitted). The Relevance of Sport in the Lives of Refugee Athletes after Their Resettlement. *Z'Flucht*.
4. Michelini, E. (2021). The Representation of the 'Refugee Crisis' and 'Sport' in the German Press: An Analysis of Newspaper Discourse. *European Journal for Sport and Society*, 18(3), 265–282. doi:10.1080/16138171.2021.1930945
5. Michelini, E. (2021). The Representation of Yusra Mardini as a Refugee Olympic Athlete: A Sociological Analysis. *Sport und Gesellschaft*, 18(1), 39–64. doi: 10.1515/sug-2021-0003
6. Michelini, E. (2022). Organised Sport in Refugee Sites: An Ethnographic Research in Niamey. *European Journal for Sport and Society*, 19(1), 1–17. doi:10.1080/16138171.2021.1878433
7. Michelini, E. (2020). Coping with Sport Ambitions after Forced Migration: Strategies of Refugee Athletes. *European Journal for Sport and Society*, 17(4), 345–361. doi:10.1080/16138171.2020.1792114
8. Michelini, E. (2020). Refugees, Physical Activity and Sport. A Systematic Literature Review. *Mondi Migranti*, 14(3), 131–152. doi:10.3280/MM2020-003008
9. Tuchel, J., Burrmann, U., Nobis, T., Michelini, E., & Schlesinger, T. (2021). Practices of Voluntary Sports Clubs to Include Refugees. *Sport in Society*, 24(4), 670–692. doi:10.1080/17430437.2019.1706491

---

* These peer-reviewed journal articles are ordered chronologically and appear in the bibliography of this habilitation, which also contains additional publications by the author.

10 Michelini, E., Burrmann, U., Nobis, T., Tuchel, J., & Schlesinger, T. (2018). Sport Offers for Refugees in Germany. Promoting and Hindering Conditions in Voluntary Sport Clubs. *Society Register, 2*(1), 19–38. doi: 10.14746/sr.2018.2.1.02

11 Michelini, E. (2018). War, Migration, Resettlement and Sport Socialization of Young Athletes: The Case of Syrian Elite Water Polo. *European Journal for Sport and Society, 15*(1), 5–21. doi: 10.1080/16138171.2018.1440949

References

Abd Rahim, B. H., Diah, N. M., & Aman, M. S. (2018). From Immigrants to Sports Figures: The Case Study of the IOC Refugee Team in Rio Olympics 2016. *Al-Shajarah, 23*(Special Issue: Migration and Refugee Studies 2018), 137–154. https://journals.iium.edu.my/shajarah/index.php/shaj/article/view/740.

Abdi, A. M. (2005). In Limbo: Dependency, Insecurity, and Identity amongst Somali Refugees in Dadaab Camps. *Refuge: Canada's Journal on Refugees, 22*(2), 6–14.

Afifi, Z. E. M. (1997). Daily Practices, Study Performance and Health during the Ramadan Fast. *Journal of the Royal Society of Health, 117*(4), 231–235. 10.1177/146642409711700406

Agamben, G. (1998). *Homo Sacer: Sovereign Power and Bare Life*. Stanford: Stanford University Press.

Ager, A., & Strang, A. (2008). Understanding Integration: A Conceptual Framework. *Journal of Refugee Studies, 21*(2), 166–191. 10.1093/jrs/fen016

Agergaard, S. (2008). Elite Athletes as Migrants in Danish Women's Handball. *International Review for the Sociology of Sport, 43*(1), 5–19. 10.11 77/1012690208093471

Agergaard, S. (2018). *Rethinking Sports and Integration: Developing a Transnational Perspective on Migrants and Descendants in Sports*. London: Routledge.

Agergaard, S. (2019). Nationalising Minority Ethnic Athletes: Danish Media Representations of Nadia Nadim around the UEFA Women's Euro 2017. *Sport in History, 39*(2), 130–146. 10.1080/17460263.2019.1608849

Agergaard, S., & Engh, M. H. (2017). Globalization, Migration and race in sport. In J. Nauright & D. K. Wiggins (Eds.), *Routledge Handbook of Sport, Race and Ethnicity* (pp. 107–120). Abingdon: Routledge.

Agergaard, S., Michelsen la Cour, A., & Gregersen, M. T. (2016). Politicisation of Migrant Leisure: A Public and Civil Intervention Involving Organised Sports. *Leisure Studies, 35*(2), 200–214. 10.1080/02614367.2015. 1009848

Agergaard, S., & Ryba, T. V. (2014). Migration and Career Transitions in Professional Sports: Transnational Athletic Careers in a Psychological and

References

Sociological Perspective. *Sociology of Sport Journal, 31*(2), 228–247. 10.1123/ssj.2013-0031

Agier, M. (2008). *On the Margins of the World: The Refugee Experience Today*. Cambridge: Polity.

Ainsworth, B. E., Haskell, W. L., Whitt, M. C., Irwin, M. L., Swartz, A. M., Strath, S. J., ... Leon, A. S. (2000). Compendium of Physical Activities: An Update of Activity Codes and MET Intensities. *Medicine & Science in Sports & Exercise, 32*(9 Suppl.), 498–516. doi:0195-9131/00/3209-0498/0

Akpınar, L., & Wagner, C. (2019). Die Darstellung von Flucht und Migration in der deutschen Presse (2015) [The Representation of Flight and Migration in the Geman Media (2015)]. In E. Arslan & K. Bozay (Eds.), *Symbolische Ordnung und Flüchtlingsbewegungen in der Einwanderungsgesellschaft* (pp. 299–323). Wiesbaden: Springer.

Alba, R., & Nee, V. (1997). Rethinking Assimilation Theory for a New Era of Immigration. *International Migration Review, 31*(4), 826–874.

Albert, K., & Nobis, T. (2020). Das Projekt Studierendenfachtagung "Integration und Sport". In C. Wulf, S. Haberstroh, & M. Petersen (Eds.), *Forschendes Lernen: Theorie, Empirie, Praxis* (pp. 298–307). Wiesbaden: Springer.

Algan, Y., Guriev, S., Papaioannou, E., & Passari, E. (2017). The European Trust Crisis and the Rise of Populism. *Brookings Papers on Economic Activity, 2017*(2), 309–400.

Aljazeera. (2016). Syria's Civil War Explained. *Aljazeera*. http://www.aljazeera.com/news/2016/05/syria-civil-war-explained-160505084119966.html

Aljazeera. (2018). Syria's Civil War Explained from the Beginning. *Aljazeera*. https://www.aljazeera.com/news/2016/05/syria-civil-war-explained-160505084119966.html

Amnesty International. (2016). EU-Turkey Refugee Deal a Historic Blow to Rights. https://www.amnesty.org/en/latest/news/2016/03/eu-turkey-refugee-deal-a-historic-blow-to-rights/

Andrews, D. L. (1993). Desperately seeking Michel: Foucault's genealogy, the body, and critical sport sociology. *Sociology of Sport Journal, 10*(2), 148–167.

Aristotle. (350 BCE/1932). *Politics* (H. Rackham, Trans. Vol. 21). Cambridge: Harvard University Press.

Arribas-Ayllon, M., & Walkerdine, V. (2008). Foucauldian Discourse Analysis. In C. Willig (Ed.), *The Sage Handbook of Qualitative Research in Psychology* (pp. 91–108). Los Angeles: Sage.

Ashby, W. R. (1991). Requisite Variety and Its Implications for the Control of Complex Systems. In G. J. Klir (Ed.), *Facets of systems science* (pp. 405–417). New York: Springer.

Asylum Information Database. (2017). Accelerated, Prioritised and Fast-track Asylum Procedures: Legal Frameworks and Practice in Europe. https://www.ecre.org/wp-content/uploads/2017/05/AIDA-Brief_AcceleratedProcedures.pdf

Back, L., Crabbe, T., & Solomos, J. (1999). Beyond the Racist/Hooligan Couplet: Race, Social Theory and Football Culture. *British Journal of Sociology, 50*(3), 419–442. 10.1111/j.1468-4446.1999.00419.x

References 97

Bade, K. (2008). *Migration in European History* (A. Brown, Trans.). Malden: Blackwell.

Bairner, A. (2012). For a sociology of sport. *Sociology of Sport Journal, 29*(1), 102–117. 10.1123/ssj.29.1.102

Baker, P., Gabrielatos, C., Khosravinik, M., Krzyżanowski, M., McEnery, T., & Wodak, R. (2008). A Useful Methodological Synergy? Combining Critical Discourse Analysis and Corpus Linguistics to Examine Discourses of Refugees and Asylum Seekers in the UK Press. *Discourse & Society, 19*(3), 273–306. 10.1177/0957926508088962

Baraldi, C., Corsi, G., & Esposito, E. (1997). *Luhmann in glossario. I concetti fondamentali della teoria dei sistemi sociali* [Glossary of Niklas Luhmann's Systems Theory] (2nd ed.). Milano: Franco Angeli.

Barbot, O. (2020). George Floyd and Our Collective Moral Injury. *AJPH, 110*(9), 1253. 10.2105/AJPH.2020.305850

BBC. (2016a). Gambia Goalkeeper Dies Trying to Reach Europe. *BBC*. https://www.bbc.com/news/world-africa-37858611

BBC. (2016b). Paris Attacks: Who Were the Attackers? *BBC*. https://www.bbc.com/news/world-europe-34832512

BBC. (2016c). Syria: The Story of the Conflict. *BBC*. http://www.bbc.com/news/world-middle-east-26116868

BBC. (2019). Why Is There a War in Syria? *BBC*. https://www.bbc.com/news/world-middle-east-35806229

Becatoros, E. (2019). 3 years on, what's become of the EU-Turkey migration deal? *AP News*. https://apnews.com/2eb94ba9aee14272bd99909be2325e2b

Berry, J. W. (2015). Acculturation. In J. E. Grusec & P. D. Hastings (Eds.), *Handbook of Socialization: Theory and Research* (pp. 520–538). New York: Guilford.

Berry, J. W., Kim, U., Minde, T., & Mok, D. (1987). Comparative Studies of Acculturative Stress. *International Migration Review, 21*(3), 491–511. 10.2307/2546607

Bertalanffy, L. V. (1968). *General System Theory*. New York: Braziller.

Besteman, C. (2016). *Making Refuge. Somali Bantu Refugees and Lewiston, Maine*. Durham: Duke University Press.

Bette, K.-H. (1989). *Körperspuren: zur Semantik und Paradoxie moderner Körperlichkeit* [Body Marks: The Paradox and Semantic of Modern Physicality] (2 ed.). Berlin: de Gruyter.

Bette, K.-H. (1995). Sport and Individualization. In K.-H. Bette & A. Rütten (Eds.), *International Sociology of Sport: Contemporary Issues* (pp. 33–44). Stuttgart: Naglschmid.

Bette, K.-H. (2010). *Sportsoziologie*. Bielfeld: Transcript.

Bette, K.-H. (2019). *Sporthelden* [Sport Heroes]. Bielefeld: transcript.

Bette, K.-H., & Gugutzer, R. (2012). Sport als Sucht. Zur Soziologie einer stoffungebundenen Abhängigkeit. [Sport as an Addiction. On the Sociology of a Substance-Independent Dependency]. *Sport und Gesellschaft, 9*(2), 107–130. 10.1515/sug-2012-0202

References

Bette, K.-H., & Kutsch, T. (1981). Doping im Sport [Doping in Elite Sports]. In T. Kutsch & G. Wiswede (Eds.), *Sport und Gesellschaft. Die Kehrseite der Medaille* (pp. 104–114). Königstein: Nain.

Bette, K.-H., & Schimank, U. (2006). *Doping im Hochleistungssport: Anpassung durch Abweichung* [Doping in Competitive Sports: Adaptation Through Deviation] (2nd ed.). Frankfurt am Main: Suhrkamp.

Betts, A. (2013). *Survival migration: Failed governance and the crisis of displacement*. Ithaca: Cornell University Press.

Betts, A. (Ed.) (2011). *Global Migration Governance*. Oxford: Oxford University Press.

Betts, A., & Collier, P. (2017). *Refuge: Transforming a broken refugee system*. London: Penguin.

Beutler, I. (2008). Sport Serving Development and Peace: Achieving the Goals of the United Nations through Sport. *Sport in Society, 11*(4), 359–369. 10.1080/17430430802019227

Biggs, D., Biggs, R., Dakos, V., Scholes, R. J., & Schoon, M. (2011). Are We Entering an Era of Concatenated Global Crises? *Ecology and Society, 16*(2), [online].

Binder, S., & Tošić, J. (2005). Refugees as a Particular Form of Transnational Migrations and Social Transformations: Socioanthropological and Gender Aspects. *Current Sociology, 53*(4), 607–624. 10.1177/0011392105052717

Black, R. (2001). Fifty years of refugee studies: From theory to policy. *International Migration Review, 35*(1), 57–78.

Block, K., & Gibbs, L. (2017). Promoting Social Inclusion Through Sport for Refugee-Background Youth in Australia: Analysing Different Participation Models. *Social inclusion, 5*(2), 91–100. 10.17645/si.v5i2.903

Boesen, I. W. (1985). From Autonomy to Dependency: Aspects of the 'Dependency Syndrome' among Afghan Refugees. *Migration Today, 13*(5), 17–21.

Bohnsack, R., Nentwig-Gesemann, I., & Nohl, A.-M. (2013). *Die dokumentarische Methode und ihre Forschungspraxis: Grundlagen qualitativer Sozialforschung* [The Documentary Method and its Research Practice: Fundaments of Qualitative Social Research]. Wiesbaden: Springer.

Bond, P. (2015). Global Crisis, African Oppression (2001). In J. T. Roberts, A. B. Hite, & N. Chorev (Eds.), *The Globalization and Development Reader: Perspectives on Development and Global Change* (pp. 345–356). West Sussex: Blackwell.

Borch, C. (2011). *Niklas Luhmann*. London: Taylor & Francis.

Bortoletto, N., Michelini, E., & Porrovecchio, A. (2021). Editorial: Sport in the Context of Migration and Health Crises. *Italian Sociological Review, 11*(5), 573–584. 10.13136/isr.v11i5S.472

Bouchard, C., & Shephard, R. J. (1994). Physical activity, Fitness, and Health: The Model and Key Concepts. In C. Bouchard, R. J. Shephard, & T. Stephens (Eds.), *Physical Activity, Fitness, and Health. International Proceedings and Consensus Statement* (pp. 77–88). Champaign: Human Kinetics.

Bowen, G. A. (2009). Document analysis as a qualitative research method. *Qualitative research journal, 9*(2), 27–40. 10.3316/QRJ0902027

Boyd, A. (1994). *Broadcast Journalism, Techniques of Radio and TV News*. Oxford: Focal.

Bradley, J. (1993). Methodological issues and practices in qualitative research. *The Library Quarterly, 63*(4), 431–449.

Brändle, V. K., Eisele, O., & Trenz, H.-J. (2019). Contesting European Solidarity during the "Refugee Crisis": A Comparative Investigation of Media Claims in Denmark, Germany, Greece and Italy. *Mass Communication and Society, 22*(6), 708–732. 10.1080/15205436.2019.1674877

Braun, S. (2011). Assoziative Lebenswelt, bindendes Sozialkapital und Migrantenvereine in Sport und Gesellschaft. In S. Braun & T. Nobis (Eds.), *Migration, Integration und Sport* (pp. 29–43). Wiesbaden: Springer.

Braun, S. (2018). "Integration durch Sport" - Ergebnisse der wissenschaftlichen Begleitung. https://cdn.dosb.de/user_upload/www.integration-durchsport.de/Service/Info-Material/IdS_Ergebnisbroschuere_Wiss._Begleitung_ 2015-2017.pdf

Braun, S., & Finke, S. (2010). *Integrationsmotor Sportverein: Ergebnisse zum Modellprojekt "spin-sport interkulturell"*. Wiesbaden: Springer.

Braun, S., & Nobis, T. (2011). *Migration, Integration und Sport* [Integration, Migration and Sport]. Wiesbaden: Springer.

Braun, V., & Clarke, V. (2012). Thematic Analysis. In H. Cooper & American Psychological Association (Eds.), *APA Handbook of Research Methods in Psychology* (pp. 57–71). Washington, DC: Magination.

Breuer, C. (2017). Sportvereine, Sportbünde und Flüchtlinge. In C. Breuer, S. Feiler, & T. Nowy (Eds.), *Sportentwicklungsbericht 2015/2016: Analyse zur Situation der Sportvereine in Deutschland* (pp. 47–100). Hellenthal: Strauß.

Breuer, C., Hoekman, R., Nagel, S., & van der Werff, H. (Eds.). (2015). *Sport clubs in Europe: A Cross-National Comparative Perspective*. Cham: Springer.

Brunner, O., Conze, W., & Koselleck, R. (1972–1997). *Geschichtliche Grundbegriffe. Historisches Lexikon zur politisch-sozialen Sprache in Deutschland* [Basic Concepts in History: A Historical Dictionary of Political and Social Language in Germany]. Stuttgart: Klett-Cotta.

Burdsey, D. (2016). One Guy Named Mo: Race, Nation and the London 2012 Olympic Games. *Sociology of Sport Journal, 33*(1), 14–25. 10.1123/ssj.2015-0009

Burdsey, D., Michelini, E., & Agergaard, S. (2022). Beyond crisis? Institutionalised mediatization of the Refugee Olympic Team at the 2020 Olympic Games. *Communication and Sport*. 10.1177/21674795221110232

Burrmann, U. (2017). Integration von geflüchteten Heranwachsenden im und durch (Schul-)Sport?! *Sportunterricht, 66*(6), 163–168.

Burrmann, U. (2020). Sportvereine als Orte lokaler Zugehörigkeit für Jugendliche mit Migrationshintergrund? *RdJB Recht der Jugend und des Bildungswesens, 67*(4), 331–343. 10.5771/0034-1312-2019-4-331

100 References

Burrmann, U., Brandmann, K., & Chudaske, F. (2015). "Wir sind ja in unserer wirklich eigenen Welt, wir haben unseren Sport.": Anforderungen und Bewältigungsprozesse im Nachwuchsleistungssport bei Jugendlichen mit Migrationshintergrund [Youth, Migration and Sport: Cultural Differences and the Socialisation in Sport Organisations]. In U. Burrmann, M. Mutz, & U. Zender (Eds.), *Jugend, Migration und Sport: Kulturelle Unterschiede und die Sozialisation zum Vereinssport* (pp. 313–338). Wiesbaden: Springer.

Burrmann, U., Brandmann, K., Mutz, M., & Zender, U. (2017). Ethnic Identities, Sense of Belonging and the Significance of Sport: Stories from Immigrant Youths in Germany. *European Journal for Sport and Society*, *14*(3), 186–204. 10.1080/16138171.2017.1349643

Burrmann, U., Mutz, M., & Zender, U. (2015a). Sportvereinsbezogene Sozialisation von Jugendlichen mit Migrationshintergrund: Zusammenfassung und Ausblick [Youth, Migration and Sport: Cultural Differences and the Socialisation in Sport Organisations]. In U. Burrmann, M. Mutz, & U. Zender (Eds.), *Jugend, Migration und Sport: Kulturelle Unterschiede und die Sozialisation zum Vereinssport* (pp. 375–384). Wiesbaden: Springer.

Burrmann, U., Mutz, M., & Zender, U. (Eds.). (2015b). *Jugend, Migration und Sport: Kulturelle Unterschiede und die Sozialisation zum Vereinssport*. [Youth, Migration and Sport: Cultural Differences and the Socialisation in Sport Organisations]. Wiesbaden: Springer.

Burrmann, U., Neuber, N., Michelini, E., Quade, S., & Brandmann, K. (2019). Abschlussbericht zur wissenschaftlichen Begleitung der dsj-Projekte "Orientierung durch Sport" (OdS 1 und 2). Frankfurt: dsj. https://www.dsj.de/fileadmin/user_upload/Bericht_Wissenschafltiche_Belgeitung.pdf

Burrmann, U., Rübner, A., Braun, S., Nobis, T., Langner, R., Mutz, M., ... Rickert, M. (2014). Ziele, Konzepte und Wirkungen sportbezogener Integrationsarbeit aus Sicht der Funktionsträger/-innen des DOSB-Programms „Integration durch Sport". http://www.integration-durch-sport.de/fileadmin/fm-dosb/arbeitsfelder/ids/files/downloads_pdf/downloads_2014/Evaluation_Programm_Integration_durch_Sport_2013.pdf

Cachay, K. (1988). *Sport und Gesellschaft: Zur Ausdifferenzierung einer Funktion und ihrer Folgen* [Sport and Society: On the Differentiation of a Function and Its Consequences]. Schorndorf: Hofmann.

Cachay, K. (1990). Versportlichung der Gesellschaft und Entsportung des Sports - Systemtheoretische Anmerkungen zu einem gesellschaftlichen Phänomen [The Sportification of Society and the De-Sportification of Sport - Systems Theoretical Reflections on a Social Phenomenon]. In H. Gabler & U. Göhner (Eds.), *Für einen besseren Sport* (pp. 97–113). Schorndorf: Hofmann.

Cachay, K., & Thiel, A. (2000). *Soziologie des Sports: Zur Ausdifferenzierung und Entwicklungsdynamik des Sports der modernen Gesellschaft* [Sociology of Sport: On the Differentiation and Dynamics of the Development of Sport in Modern Society]. Weinheim: Juventa.

References 101

Campante, F., & Yanagizawa-Drott, D. (2015). Does Religion Affect Economic Growth and Happiness? Evidence from Ramadan. *The Quarterly Journal of Economics, 130*(2), 615–658. 10.1093/qje/qjv002

Caperchione, C. M., Kolt, G. S., & Mummery, W. K. (2009). Physical Activity in Culturally and Linguistically Diverse Migrant Groups to Western Society. *Sports Medicine, 39*(3), 167–177. 10.2165/00007256-200939030-00001

Caperchione, C. M., Kolt, G. S., Tennent, R., & Mummery, W. K. (2011). Physical Activity Behaviours of Culturally and Linguistically Diverse (CALD) Women Living in Australia: A Qualitative Study of Socio-Cultural Influences. *BMC Public Health, 11*(1), 26.

Carastathis, A., Spathopoulou, A., & Tsilimpounidi, M. (2018). Crisis, what crisis? Immigrants, refugees, and invisible struggles. *Refuge: Canada's Journal on Refugees/Refuge: revue canadienne sur les réfugiés, 34*(1), 29–38. 10.7202/1050852ar

Carlson, M., Jakli, L., & Linos, K. (2018). Rumors and refugees: how government-created information vacuums undermine effective crisis management. *International Studies Quarterly, 62*(3), 671–685. 10.1093/isq/sqy018

Carter, T. (2011). *In Foreign fields: The politics and experiences of transnational sport migration*. London: Pluto Press.

Caspersen, C. J., Powell, K. E., & Christenson, G. M. (1985). Physical activity, exercise, and physical fitness: definitions and distinctions for health-related research. *Public Health Reports, 100*(2), 126–131.

Castles, S. (2003). Towards a Sociology of Forced Migration and Social Transformation. *Sociology, 37*(1), 13–34. 10.1177/0038038503037001384

Castles, S., De Haas, H., & Miller, M. (2014). *The age of migration: International population movements in the modern world* (5 ed.). Houndmills: Palgrave Macmillan.

Castles, S., Korac, M., Vasta, E., & Vertovec, S. (2002). *Integration: Mapping the field*. London: The University of Oxford Centre for Migration and Policy Research and Refugee Studies Centre.

Cavill, N., Kahlmeier, S., & Racioppi, F. (2006). *Physical Activity and Health in Europe: Evidence for Action*. Geneve: World Health Organization.

Çelebi, E., Verkuyten, M., & Bagci, S. C. (2017). Ethnic identification, discrimination, and mental and physical health among Syrian refugees: The moderating role of identity needs. *European journal of social psychology, 47*(7), 832–843. 10.1002/ejsp.2299

Chauzy, J.-P., & Appave, G. (2013). Communicating effectively about migration. In G. Dell'Orto & V. L. Birchfield (Eds.), *Reporting at the Southern borders: Journalism and public debates on immigration in the US and the EU* (pp. 62–72). New York: Routledge.

Chomsky, N. (1971). Human nature: justice versus power. Noam Chomsky debates with Michel Foucault. https://chomsky.info/1971xxxx/

Chugh, A. (2020). Will COVID-19 Change how we Think about Migration and Migrant Workers? *World Economic Forum*. https://www.weforum.org/agenda/2020/05/covid-19-coronavirus-migration-migrant-workers-immigration-policy-health-securitization-risk-travel-bubbles/

References

CNN. (2016). Syrian Civil War Fast Facts. *CNN.* http://edition.cnn.com/2013/08/27/world/meast/syria-civil-war-fast-facts/
CNN. (2020). Syria Crisis. *CNN.* https://edition.cnn.com/specials/middleeast/syria
Coakley, J., & Dunning, E. (2000). *Handbook of Sports Studies.* London: SAGE.
Coalter, F. (2008). Sport-in-development: Development for and through Sport? In M. Nicholson & R. Hoye (Eds.), *Sport and Social Capital* (pp. 39–67). Oxford: Elsevier.
Cole, C. L., Giardina, M. D., & Andrews, D. L. (2004). Michel Foucault: Studies of power and sport. In R. Giulianotti (Ed.), *Sport and modern social theorists* (pp. 207–223). London: Springer.
Coleman, J. S. (1994). *Foundations of Social Theory.* Cambridge: Harvard University Press.
Collins, P. H., & Bilge, S. (2020). *Intersectionality* (2 ed.). Cambridge: Polity.
Cooke, J. G., & Sanderson, T. M. (2016). *Militanc and the Arc of Instability. Violent Extremism in the Sahel.* Lanham: Rowman & Littlefield.
Cooper, S., Olejniczak, E., Lenette, C., & Smedley, C. (2017). Media coverage of refugees and asylum seekers in regional Australia: a critical discourse analysis. *Media International Australia, 162*(1), 78–89. 10.1177/1329878X16667832
Council of Europe. (2020). Integrating Migrants and Refugees: The Role of Sport. https://www.coe.int/en/web/sport/home
Craig, P. (2016). *Sport Sociology* (3 ed.). London: SAGE.
Cranmer, G. A., & Goodboy, A. K. (2015). Power play: Coach power use and athletes' communicative evaluations and responses. *Western Journal of Communication, 79*(5), 614–633. 10.1080/10570314.2015.1069389
Creswell, J. W., & Creswell, J. D. (2017). *Research design: Qualitative, quantitative, and mixed methods approaches.* Los Angeles: SAGE.
Cullum, B. (2021). Tokyo 2020: Tegla Loroupe's concerns over Olympic Refugee Team. *BBC.* https://www.bbc.com/sport/africa/56689800
Dany, F., Mallon, M., & Arthur, M. (2003). The Odyssey of Career and the Opportunity for International Comparison. *International Journal of Human Resource Management, 14*(5), 705–712. 10.1080/0958519032000080758
Darby, P. (2013). *Africa, football and FIFA: politics, colonialism and resistance.* London: Cass.
Darby, P., Akindes, G., & Kirwin, M. (2007). Football academies and the migration of African football labor to Europe. *Journal of Sport and Social Issues, 31*(2), 143–161. 10.1177/0193723507300481
Darnell, S. C. (2012). *Sport for Development and Peace: A Critical Sociology.* New York: Bloomsbury.
De Martini Ugolotti, N., & Caudwell, J. (Eds.). (2021). *Leisure and Forced Migration: Lives Lived in Asylum Systems.* London: Routledge.
Delaney, T., & Madigan, T. (2009). Socialization and Sport. In T. Delaney & T. Madigan (Eds.), *The Sociology of Sports: An Introduction* (pp. 77–95). Jefferson and London: McFarland.

References

Digel, H. (1990). Die Versportlichung unserer Kultur und deren Folgen für den Sport - Ein Beitrag zur Uneigentlichkeit des Sports [The Sportification of our Culture and its Impact on Sport - An Essay on the Inauthenticity of Sport]. In H. Gabler & U. Göhner (Eds.), *Für einen besseren Sport* (pp. 73–96). Schorndorf: Hofmann.

Dockery, W. (2017). Two years since Germany opened its borders to refugees: A chronology. *Deutsche Welle*. https://www.dw.com/en/two-years-since-germany-opened-its-borders-to-refugees-a-chronology/a-40327634

Doidge, M., & Sandri, E. (2019). 'Friends that last a lifetime': the importance of emotions amongst volunteers working with refugees in Calais. *The British journal of sociology*, 70(2), 463–480. 10.1111/1468-4446.12484

Dowling, F. (2020). A Critical Discourse Analysis of a Local Enactment of Sport for Integration Policy: Helping Young Refugees or Self-Help for Voluntary Sports Clubs? *International Review for the Sociology of Sport*, 55(8), 1152–1166. 10.1177/1012690219874437

dsj. (2020). Orientierung durch Sport. https://www.dsj.de/ods/

Duden. (2020). -ling. https://www.duden.de/rechtschreibung/_ling

Dussel, E. (1995). *The Invention of the Americas: Eclipse of 'the Other' and the Myth of Modernity* (M. D. Barber, Trans.). New York: Continuum.

Eberl, J.-M., Meltzer, C. E., Heidenreich, T., Herrero, B., Theorin, N., Lind, F., ... Strömbäck, J. (2018). The European Media Discourse on Immigration and its Effects: A Literature Review. *Annals of the International Communication Association*, 42(3), 207–223. 10.1080/23808985.2018.1497452

Eckstein, H. (1975). Case study and theory in political science. In F. I. Greenstein & N. W. Polsby (Eds.), *Strategies of Inquiry* (Vol. 7, pp. 79–137). Reading: Addison-Wesley.

Economist, T. (2020, 2020-11-28). Africa's do-or-die boat people. West Africans are dying trying to reach the Canary Islands. *The Economist*. https://www.economist.com/middle-east-and-africa/2020/11/28/west-africans-are-dying-trying-to-reach-the-canary-islands

Elling, A., Knoppers, A., & De Knop, P. (2001). The Social Integrative Meaning of Sport: A Critical and Comparative Analysis of Policy and Practice in the Netherlands. *Sociology of Sport Journal*, 18, 414–434. 10.1123/ssj.18.4.414

Engel, S., Deuter, M.-S., Mantel, A., Noack, M., Wohlert, J., & Raspel, J. (2019). Die (Re) Produktion symbolischer Ordnung–Narrative in der deutschen Medienberichterstattung über Flucht und Geflüchtete [The (Re-) Production of Symbolic Order Narrative in German Media Coverage of Refugees]. In E. Arslan & K. Bozay (Eds.), *Symbolische Ordnung und Flüchtlingsbewegungen in der Einwanderungsgesellschaft* (pp. 273–298). Wiesbaden: Springer.

Engels, F. (1844/1996). Outlines of a Critique of Political Economy (M. Milligan, Trans.). In A. Ruge & K. Marx (Eds.), *German-French Annals* (Vol. 1). Paris: Office of the Annals.

References

Engin, K. (2017). A year of loneliness on Greek Islands: The EU-Turkey refugee agreement. *The Jerusalem Post*. https://www.jpost.com/Opinion/A-year-of-loneliness-on-Greek-Islands-The-EU-Turkey-refugee-agreement-484290

ENGSO. (2020). ASPIRE - Activity, Sport, Play for the Inclusion of Refugees. https://www.aspiresport.eu/

Escobar, A. (1984). Discourse and power in development: Michel Foucault and the relevance of his work to the Third World. *Alternatives, 10*(3), 377–400.

Esser, H. (1993). *Soziologie: Allgemeine Grundlagen*. Frankfurt: Campus.

Esser, H. (2006). *Migration, Sprache und Integration*. Berlin: Wissenschaftszentrum Berlin für Sozialforschung.

European Commission. (2007). White Paper on Sport. https://eur-lex.europa.eu/legal-content/EN/TXT/PDF/?uri=CELEX:52007DC0391&from=EN

European Council, & Turkey. (2016). EU-Turkey Deal. https://www.consilium.europa.eu/en/press/press-releases/2016/03/18/eu-turkey-statement/

European Union. (2020). The EU in brief. https://europa.eu/european-union/about-eu/eu-in-brief_en

Eurostat. (2020). Asylum statistics. https://ec.europa.eu/eurostat/statistics-explained/index.php/Asylum_statistics

Evans, A. B., Agergaard, S., Campbell, P. I., Hylton, K., & Lenneis, V. (2020). 'Black Lives Matter:' sport, race and ethnicity in challenging times. *European Journal for Sport and Society, 17*(4), 289–300. 10.1080/16138171.2020.1833499

Evans, A. B., Blackwell, J., Dolan, P., Fahlén, J., Hoekman, R., Lenneis, V., … Wilcock, L. (2020). Sport in the Face of the COVID-19 Pandemic: Towards an Agenda for Research in the Sociology of Sport. *European Journal for Sport and Society, 17*(2), 85–95. 10.1080/16138171.2020.1765100

Fahn, K. (2019). *Integrationswirkungen des Sports für Geflüchtete - Eine qualitative Inhaltsanalyse von Zeitungsartikeln aus den Jahren 2015 und 2016*. (Master). TU Dortmund.

Farah, M. (2013). *Twin Ambitions - My Autobiography*. London: Hodder.

Farooq, S., & Parker, A. (2009). Sport, Physical Education, and Islam: Muslim Independent Schooling and the Social Construction of Masculinities. *Sociology of Sport Journal, 26*(2), 277–295. 10.1123/ssj.26.2.277

Faulstich, W. (Ed.) (2000). *Grundwissen Medien*. [Basic Knowledge of Media]. München: Fink.

Feuchter, M., & Janetzko, A. (2018). "Refugees Welcome in Sports" - Bewegungsangebote für Geflüchtete im Spannungsfeld zwischen Integrationsforderung und Partizipationszwang. ["Refugees Welcome in Sports" - Physical Activity Offers for Refugees between Demand for Integration and Compulsory Participation]. *Sport und Gesellschaft, 15*(2–3), 125–157. 10.1515/sug-2018-0008

Fiddian-Qasmiyeh, E. (2016). Representations of displacement from the Middle East and North Africa. *Public Culture, 28*(3), 457–473. 10.1215/08992363-3511586

References

Flick, U. (2011). *Triangulation: Eine Einführung* [Triangulation: An Introduction] (3rd ed.). Wiesbaden: VS.

Fong, E., & Li, J. X. (2017). Migration. *Oxford Bibliographies*, online. https://www.oxfordbibliographies.com/view/document/obo-9780199756384/obo-9780199756384-0128.xml

Fotopoulos, S., & Kaimaklioti, M. (2016). Media Discourse on the Refugee Crisis: On What Have the Greek, German and British Press Focused? *European View, 15*(2), 265–279. 10.1007/s12290-016-0407-5

Foucault, M. (1972). *The Archaeology of Knowledge* (A. M. Sheridan Smith, Trans.). London: Routledge.

Foucault, M. (1977). *Discipline and Punish. The Birth of the Prison* (A. Sheridan, Trans.). New York: Random House.

Foucault, M. (1990). *The History of Sexuality* (R. Hurley, Trans. Vol. 1: An Introduction). New York: Vintage.

Fox, R. (2001). Constructivism examined. *Oxford Review of Education, 27*(1), 23–35. 10.1080/03054980020030583

Freedman, J. (2016). Sexual and gender-based violence against refugee women: a hidden aspect of the refugee "crisis". *Reproductive Health Matters, 24*(47), 18–26. 10.1016/j.rhm.2016.05.003

Fry, L. (2015). Refugee crisis timeline: How the crisis has grown. *Independent*. https://www.independent.co.uk/news/world/europe/refugee-crisis-timeline-how-crisis-has-grown-10502690.html

Fuchs-Heinritz, W. (2010). Biographieforschung [Biography Research]. In G. Kneer & M. Schroer (Eds.), *Handbuch Spezielle Soziologien* (pp. 85–104). Wiesbaden: Springer.

Gadamer, H.-G. (1960/2004). *Truth and Method* (2 ed.). New York: Continuum.

Geels, F. W. (2002). Technological transitions as evolutionary reconfiguration processes: a multi-level perspective and a case-study. *Research policy, 31*(8–9), 1257–1274.

Georgiou, M., & Zaborowski, R. (2017). *Media Coverage of the "Refugee Crisis": A Cross-European Perspective*. Strasbourg: Council of Europe.

German Federal Government. (2007). *Der Nationaler Integrationsplan*. Berlin: German Federal Government.

Ghorashi, H. (2008). Giving Silence a Chance: The Importance of Life Stories for Research on Refugees. *Journal of Refugee Studies, 21*(1), 117–132. 10.1093/jrs/fem033

Giulianotti, R. (2011). The Sport, Development and Peace Sector: A Model of four Social Policy Domains. *Journal of Social Policy, 40*(4), 757–776. 10.1017/S0047279410000930

Giulianotti, R. (Ed.) (2015). *Routledge handbook of the sociology of sport*. London and New York: Routledge.

Giulianotti, R., & Armstrong, G. (2013). The Sport for Development and Peace Sector: A Critical Sociological Analysis. In N. Schulenkorf & D. Adair (Eds.), *Global Sport-for-Development* (pp. 15–32). New York: Palgrave Macmillan.

References

Giulianotti, R., & Robertson, R. (2004). The globalization of football: a study in the glocalization of the 'serious life'. *The British journal of sociology*, *55*(4), 545–568. 10.1111/j.1468-4446.2004.00037.x

Gkliati, M. (2017). The EU-Turkey Deal and the Safe Third Country Concept before the Greek Asylum Appeals Committees. *Movements. Journal for Critical Migration and Border Regime Studies*, *3*(2), 213–224.

Gläser, J., & Laudel, G. (2010). *Experteninterviews und qualitative Inhaltsanalyse als Instrumente rekonstruierender Untersuchungen* (4 ed.). Wiesbaden: VS.

Gobo, G. (2018). Upside down-reinventing research design. In U. Flick (Ed.), *The sage handbook of qualitative data collection* (pp. 65–83). London: SAGE.

Grupe, O. (1988). Menschen im Sport 2000. Von der Verantwortlichkeit der Person und der Verpflichtung der Organisation [People in sport 2000. Of the individual's responsibility and the organisation's obligation]. In K. Gieseler, O. Grupe, & K. Heinemann (Eds.), *Menschen im Sport 2000. Dokumentation des Kongresses "Menschen im Sport 2000"* (pp. 44–67). Schondorf: Hofmann.

Günther, G. (1979). Life as poly-contexturality. In G. Günther (Ed.), *Beiträge zur Grundlegung einer operationsfähigen Dialektik* (Vol. 2, pp. 283–306). Hamburg: Meiner.

Gutiérrez Rodríguez, E. (2018). The Coloniality of Migration and the "Refugee Crisis": On the Asylum-Migration Nexus, the Transatlantic White European Settler Colonialism-Migration and Racial Capitalism. *Refuge: Canada's Journal on Refugees/Refuge: revue canadienne sur les réfugiés*, *34*(1), 16–28. 10.7202/1050851ar

Ha, J.-P., & Lyras, A. (2013). Sport for Refugee Youth in a New Society: The Role of Acculturation in Sport for Development and Peace Programming. *South African Journal for Research in Sport, Physical Education and Recreation*, *35*(2), 121–140.

Haag, H., Mess, F., & Haag, G. (Eds.). (2012). *Dictionary: Sport-Physical Education-Sport Science*. Berlin: Logos.

Habermas, J. (1980). *Legitimation Crisis* (T. McCarthy, Trans. 3 ed. Vol. 519). London: Heinemann.

Hajer, M. (2003). Policy without polity? Policy analysis and the institutional void. *Policy Sciences*, *36*(2), 175–195.

Hakura, F. (2016). The EU-Turkey refugee deal solves little. *Chatham House*. https://www.chathamhouse.org/publications/twt/eu-turkey-refugee-deal-solves-little

Hammersley, M., & Atkinson, P. (2019). *Ethnography: Principles in Practice* (4 ed.). London and New York: Routledge.

Hardy, C. (2003). Refugee Determination: Power and Resistance in Systems of Foucauldian Power. *Administration & Society*, *35*(4), 462–488. 10.1177/0095399703254949

Hardy, L., Barlow, M., Evans, L., Rees, T., Woodman, T., & Warr, C. (2017). Great British Medalists: Psychosocial Biographies of Super-Elite and Elite Athletes from Olympic Sports. In V. Walsh, M. Wilson, & B. Parkin (Eds.), *Progress in Brain Research* (Vol. 232, pp. 1–119). London: Elsevier.

References 107

Harrell-Bond, B. (2002). Can Humanitarian Work with Refugees Be Humane? *Human Rights Quarterly, 24*(1), 51–85.

Hartley, L., Fleay, C., & Tye, M. E. (2017). Exploring Physical Activity Engagement and Barriers for Asylum Seekers in Australia Coping with Prolonged Uncertainty and no Right to Work. *Health & Social Care in the Community, 25*(3), 1190–1198. 10.1111/hsc.12419

Hartmann, D. (2016). *Midnight Basketball: Race, Sports, and Neoliberal Social Policy*. Chicago: University of Chicago Press.

Heim, S. (2018). Bingen: Asylbewerber Gai Nyang Tap Gatpan aus Südsudan träumt von der Teilnahme an Olympischen Spielen in Tokio 2020. *Allgemeine Zeitung*. https://www.allgemeine-zeitung.de/lokales/bingen/bingen/bingen-asylbewerber-gai-nyang-tap-gatpan-aus-sudsudan-traumt-von-der-teilnahme-an-olympischen-spielen-in-tokio-2020_18932824

Heinemann, K. (1998). *Einführung in die Soziologie des Sports* [Introduction to the sociology of sport] (4th ed.). Schorndorf: Hofmann.

Heinemann, K. (2007). *Einführung in die Soziologie des Sports* [Introduction to the Sociology of Sport] (5 ed.). Schorndorf: Hofmann.

Heinrich-Böll-Stiftung (Ed.) (2016). *Welcome to Germany V – Zivilgesellschaftliches Engagement*. Berlin: Heinrich-Böll-Stiftung.

Heitmeyer, W., & Imbusch, P. (2005). *Integrationspotenziale einer modernen Gesellschaft*. Wiesbaden: Springer.

Heslop, A. (2016). Migration coverage hits saturation point. Now what? https://blog.wan-ifra.org/2016/04/19/migration-coverage-hits-saturation-point-now-what

Hesse, B., & Sayyid, S. (2006). Narrating the Postcolonial Political and Immigrant Imaginary. In N. Ali, V. S. Kalra, & S. Sayyid (Eds.), *A postcolonial people: South Asians in Britain* (pp. 13–31). London: Hurst & Co.

Hoberman, J. (2011). The Myth of Sport as a Peace-Promoting Political Force. *SAIS Review of International Affairs, 31*(1), 17–29.

Hobfoll, S. E., Spielberger, C. D., Breznitz, S., Figley, C., Folkman, S., Lepper-Green, B., ... Sarason, I. (1991). War-Related Stress: Addressing the Stress of War and Other Traumatic Events. *American Psychologist, 46*(8), 848–855. 10.1037//0003-066X.46.8.848

Holmes, S. M., & Castañeda, H. (2016). Representing the "European Refugee Crisis" in Germany and Beyond: Deservingness and Difference, Life and Death. *American Ethnologist, 43*(1), 12–24. 10.1111/amet.12259

Holton, R. J. (1987). The Idea of Crisis in Modern Society. *The British journal of sociology, 38*(4), 502–520. 10.2307/590914

Holzberg, B., Kolbe, K., & Zaborowski, R. (2018). Figures of Crisis: The Delineation of (Un) Deserving Refugees in the German Media. *Sociology, 52*(3), 534–550. 10.1177/0038038518759460

Horvath, K., & Amelina, A. (2017). Sociology of migration. In K. O. Korgen (Ed.), *The Cambridge Handbook of Sociology: Core Areas in Sociology and the Development of the Discipline* (pp. 455–464). Cambridge: Cambridge University Press.

References

Huizinga, J. (1939/2004). *Homo Ludens*. Reinbek: Rowohlt.

Hunger, U., & Kersting, N. (2019). Coping with the Challenges of Mass Migration: Reception, Distribution and Integration of Refugees in German Municipalities since 2015. *HKJU-CCPA*, *19*(3), 407–430. 10.31297/hkju.19.3.3

Hurrelmann, K. (1988). *Social Structure and Personality Development: The Individual as a Productive Processor of Reality*. Cambridge: Cambridge University Press.

Hylton, K. (2005). 'Race', sport and leisure: lessons from critical race theory. *Leisure Studies*, *24*(1), 81–98. 10.1080/02614360412331313494

Hylton, K. (2010). How a turn to critical race theory can contribute to our understanding of 'race', racism and anti-racism in sport. *International Review for the Sociology of Sport*, *45*(3), 335–354. 10.1177/1012690210371045

International Federation of Journalists. (2019). Global Charter of Ethics for Journalists. https://www.ifj.org/who/rules-and-policy/global-charter-of-ethics-for-journalists.html

Interpreter 1. (2019) *Sport at the ETM of Niamey/Interviewer: E. Michelini*.

Interpreter 2. (2019) *Sport at the ETM of Niamey/Interviewer: E. Michelini*.

Interpreter 3. (2019) *Sport at the ETM of Niamey/Interviewer: E. Michelini*.

ISA. (2020). RC38 Biography and Society. https://www.isa-sociology.org/en/research-networks/research-committees/rc38-biography-and-society/

Jackson, M. A. (2017). *Process and Emergence: A Topographic Ethnography of the Embodiment of Place and Adventure Tourism in Khumbu, Nepal*. (PhD). Prescott College, Prescott.

Jarvie, G. (Ed.) (2005). *Sport, Racism and Ethnicity*. (2 ed.). London: Falmer.

John, J. M., Gropper, H., & Thiel, A. (2019). The role of Critical Life Events in the Talent Development Pathways of Athletes and Musicians: A Systematic Review. *Psychology of Sport and Exercise*, *45*, 101565. 10.1016/j.psychsport.2019.101565

Kancs, D. A., & Lecca, P. (2018). Long-term social, economic and fiscal effects of immigration into the EU: The role of the integration policy. *The World Economy*, *41*(10), 2599–2630. 10.1111/twec.12637

Kidd, B. (2013). A New Social Movement: Sport for Development and Peace. In S. J. Jackson & S. Haigh (Eds.), *Sport and Foreign Policy in a Globalizing World* (pp. 36–46). London: Routledge.

Klein, S. E. (Ed.) (2016). *Defining Sport: Conceptions and Borderlines*. Lanham: Lexington.

Kneer, G., & Schroer, M. (Eds.). (2010). *Handbuch Spezielle Soziologien*. [Handbook of Special Sociologies]. Wiesbaden: Springer.

Kohli, R. K. (2006). The sound of silence: Listening to what unaccompanied asylum-seeking children say and do not say. *British Journal of Social Work*, *36*(5), 707–721. 10.1093/bjsw/bch305

Koopmans, R., & Pfetsch, B. (2007). Towards a Europeanised Public Sphere? Comparing Political Actors and the Media in Germany. In J. E. Fossum, P. Schlesinger, & O. K. Geir (Eds.), *Public Sphere and Civil Society? Transformations of the European Union* (pp. 57–88). Oslo: ARENA.

References 109

Koselleck, R. (1979). *Vergangene Zukunft. Zur Semantik geschichtlicher Zeiten* [Past Future. The Semantics of Historical Times]. Frankfurt: Suhrkamp.

Koselleck, R., & Richter, M. W. (2006). Crisis. *Journal of the History of Ideas*, 67(2), 357–400.

Krause, D. (2005). *Luhmann-Lexikon: Eine Einführung in das Gesamtwerk von Niklas Luhmann* [Luhmann Lexicon: An Introduction to the Complete Works of Niklas Luhmann] (4 ed.). Stuttgart: Lucius & Lucius.

Krippendorff, K. (2013). *Content Analysis: An Introduction to its Methodology* (3 ed.). London: Sage.

Krug, T. (2016). The Story of Samia Omar, the Olympic Runner who Drowned in the Med. *the Guardian*. https://www.theguardian.com/world/2016/aug/03/the-story-of-samia-omar-the-olympic-runner-who-drowned-in-the-med

Krzyżanowski, M., Triandafyllidou, A., & Wodak, R. (2018). The Mediatization and the Politicization of the "Refugee Crisis" in Europe. *Journal of Immigrant & Refugee Studies*, 16(1–2), 1–14. 10.1080/15562948.2017.1353189

Kuckartz, U., & Rädiker, S. (2019). *Analyzing qualitative data with MAXQDA*. Wiesbaden: Springer.

Kühnle, F. (2020). Sad Stories for a Better Future: Narratives and Functions of Depression Stories in Elite Athletes' Autobiographies. *European Journal for Sport and Society*, 17(3), 196–213. 10.1080/16138171.2020.1792074

Lams, L. (2018). Discursive constructions of the summer 2015 refugee crisis: A comparative analysis of French, Dutch, Belgian francophone and British centre-of-right press narratives. *Journal of Applied Journalism & Media Studies*, 7(1), 103–127. 10.1386/ajms.7.1.103_1

Land, C. (2015). *Decolonizing Solidarity: Dilemmas and Directions for Supporters of Indigenous Struggles*. London: Zed Books.

Lanfranchi, P., & Taylor, M. (2001). *Moving with the Ball: the Migration of Professional Footballers*. Oxford: Berg.

Lessa, I. (2006). Discursive Struggles within Social Welfare: Restaging Teen Motherhood. *British Journal of Social Work*, 36(2), 283–298. 10.1093/bjsw/bch256

Lewek, M., & Naber, A. (2017). Kindheit im Wartezustand – Studie zur Situation von Kindern und Jugendlichen in Flüchtlingsunterkünften in Deutschland. https://www.unicef.de/informieren/aktuelles/presse/2017/studie-fluechtlingskinder-in-deutschland/137440

Libyan Government, & Italian Government. (2017). *Memorandum d'intesa sulla cooperazione nel campo dello sviluppo, del contrasto all'immigrazione illegale, al traffico di esseri umani, al contrabbando e sul rafforzamento della sicurezza delle frontiere tra lo Stato della Libia e la Repubblica Italiana* [Memorandum of understanding on cooperation in the fields of development, the fight against illegal immigration, human trafficking and fuel smuggling and on reinforcing the security of borders between the State of Libya and the Italian Republic]. Rome: Odysseus Network.

References

Lloyd, J. (2000). Qualitative analysis: a guide to best practice. *Science & justice: journal of the Forensic Science Society, 40*(4), 278.

Lomong, L., & Tabb, M. (2012). *Running for My Life: One Lost Boy's Journey from the Killing Fields of Sudan to the Olympic Games*. Nashville: Thomas Nelson.

Loy, J. W. (1968). The nature of sport: A definitional effort. *Quest, 10*, 1–15.

Luhmann, N. (1982a). *The differentiation of society* (S. Holmes & C. Larmore, Trans.). New York: Columbia University Press.

Luhmann, N. (1982b). The World Society as a Social System. *International Journal of General Systems, 8*(3), 131–138.

Luhmann, N. (1983). Medizin und Gesellschaftstheorie. [Medicine and Social Theory]. *Medizin, Mensch, Gesellschaft, 8*, 168–175.

Luhmann, N. (1984a). The Self-Description of Society: Crisis Fashion and Sociological Theory. *International Journal of Comparative Sociology, 25*, 59–72.

Luhmann, N. (1984b). *Soziale Systeme: Grundriß einer allgemeinen Theorie* [Social Systems: Outline of a General Theory] (1st ed.). Frankfurt am Main: Suhrkamp.

Luhmann, N. (1987a). The Evolutionary Differentiation between Society and Interaction. In J. C. Alexander, B. Giesen, R. Münch, & N. J. Smelser (Eds.), *The Micro-Macro Link* (pp. 112–131). Berkeley, Los Angeles, London: University of California Press.

Luhmann, N. (1987b). *Soziale Systeme: Grundriß einer allgemeinen Theorie* [Social systems: Outline of a general theory] (1st ed.). Frankfurt am Main: Suhrkamp.

Luhmann, N. (1990). *Die Wissenschaft der Gesellschaft* [The Science of Society] (1 ed.). Frankfurt am Main: Suhrkamp.

Luhmann, N. (1997). *Die Gesellschaft der Gesellschaft* [The Society of Society] (2 ed.). Frankfurt am Main: Suhrkamp.

Luhmann, N. (2000). *The Reality of the Mass Media* (K. Cross, Trans.). Stanford: Stanford University Press.

Luhmann, N. (2005). Inklusion und Exklusion [Inclusion and Exclusion]. In N. Luhmann (Ed.), *Soziologische Aufklärung 6* (pp. 226–251). Wiesbaden: VS.

Luhmann, N. (2006). *Organisation und Entscheidung* [Organisation and Decision] (2 ed.). Wiesbaden: VS.

Luhmann, N. (2008). The Autopoiesis of Social Systems. *Journal of Sociocybernetics, 6*(2), 84–95.

Luhmann, N. (2017). *Trust and Power*. Cambridge: Polity Press.

Luhmann, N. (2018). *Organization and Decision* (R. Barrett, Trans. D. Baecker Ed.). Cambridge: Cambridge University Press.

Luhmann, N., Holmes, S., & Larmore, C. (1982). *The Differentiation of Society*. New York: Columbia University Press.

Luhmann, N., & Lenzen, D. (2002). *Das Erziehungssystem der Gesellschaft* [The Education System of Society]. Frankfurt am Main: Suhrkamp.

References 111

Maehler, D., & Brinkmann, H. U. (Eds.). (2015). *Methoden der Migrationsforschung: ein interdisziplinärer Forschungsleitfaden*. Wiesbaden: Springer.

Magee, J., & Sugden, J. (2002). "The World at their Feet" Professional Football and International Labor Migration. *Journal of Sport and Social Issues*, *26*(4), 421–437. 10.1177/0193732502238257

Maguire, J. (1996). Blade Runners: Canadian Migrants, Ice Hockey, and the Global Sports Process. *Journal of Sport and Social Issues*, *20*(3), 335–360.

Maguire, J. (2004a). Globalisation and the Making of Modern Sport. *Sportwissenschaft. The German Journal of Sports Science*, *34*(1), 7–20.

Maguire, J. (2004b). Sport Labor Migration Research Revisited. *Journal of Sport and Social Issues*, *28*(4), 477–482. 10.1177/0193723504269914

Malcolm, D. (2012). *Sport & Sociology*. London and New York: Routledge.

Maley, W. (2016). *What is a Refugee?* Oxford: Oxford University Press.

Malkki, L. H. (1995). Refugees and Exile: From 'Refugee Studies' to the National Order of Things. *Annual review of anthropology*, *24*(1), 495–523.

Malkki, L. H. (1996). Speechless emissaries: Refugees, humanitarianism, and dehistoricization. *Cultural Anthropology*, *11*(3), 377–404.

Manager 1. (2019) *Sport at the ETM of Niamey/Interviewer: E. Michelini*.

Manager 2. (2019) *Sport at the ETM of Niamey/Interviewer: E. Michelini*.

Manager 3. (2019) *Sport at the ETM of Niamey/Interviewer: E. Michelini*.

Manager 4. (2019) *Sport at the ETM of Niamey/Interviewer: E. Michelini*.

Manning, P., & Trimmer, T. (2013). *Migration in World History* (2nd ed.). London and New York: Routledge.

Mapedzahama, V., & Dune, T. (2017). A clash of paradigms? Ethnography and ethics approval. *SAGE Open*, *7*(1). doi:2158244017697167

Marcus, G. E. (1995). Ethnography in/of the world system: The emergence of multi-sited ethnography. *Annual review of anthropology*, *24*(1), 95–117.

Mardini, Y. (2018). *Butterfly: From Refugee to Olympian - My Story of Rescue, Hope, and Triumph*. London: Pan Macmillan.

Markula, P., & Pringle, R. (2006). *Foucault, sport and exercise: Power, knowledge and transforming the self*. Abingdon: Routledge.

Martin, D., Minca, C., & Katz, I. (2020). Rethinking the Camp: On Spatial Technologies of Power and Resistance. *Progress in Human Geography*, *44*(4), 743–768. 10.1177/0309132519856702

Martin, J. R. (2015). Cohesion and Texture. In D. Tannen, H. E. Hamilton, & D. Schiffrin (Eds.), *The Handbook of Discourse Analysis* (2 ed., pp. 61–81). West Sussex: Blackwell.

Marx, K. (1867/2018). *Capital. A Critique of Political Economy* (Vol. 1). Campaign: Barbarian Press.

Maslow, A. H. (1943). A theory of human motivation. *Psychological Review*, *50*(4), 370–396.

Maturana, H. R., & Varela, F. J. (1987). *The Tree of Knowledge: The Biological Roots of Human Understanding*. Boston: Shambhala.

Mauss, M. (2002). *The gift: The form and reason for exchange in archaic societies* (W. D. Halls, Trans.). London: Routledge.

References

Mayring, P. (2015). *Qualitative Inhaltsanalyse: Grundlagen und Techniken* [Qualitative Content Analysis: Principles and Techniques] (12th ed.). Weinheim: Beltz.

McGovern, P. (2002). Globalization or internationalization? Foreign footballers in the English league, 1946–95. *Sociology, 36*(1), 23–42.

Meillet, A. (1912/1965). *L'évolution des formes grammaticales* [The Evolution of Grammatic Forms]. Paris: Libraire Honoré Champion.

Michelini, E. (2018). War, Migration, Resettlement and Sport Socialization of Young Athletes: The Case of Syrian Elite Water Polo. *European Journal for Sport and Society, 15*(1), 5–21. 10.1080/16138171.2018.1440949

Michelini, E. (2020a). Coping with Sport Ambitions after Forced Migration: Strategies of Refugee Athletes. *European Journal for Sport and Society, 17*(4), 345–361. 10.1080/16138171.2020.1792114

Michelini, E. (2020b). Refugees, Physical Activity and Sport. A Systematic Literature Review. *Mondi Migranti, 14*(3), 131–152. 10.3280/MM2020-003008

Michelini, E. (2020-Submitted). The Relevance of Sport in the Lives of Refugee Athletes after their Resettlement. *Z'Flucht*.

Michelini, E. (2021a). The Representation of the 'Refugee Crisis' and 'Sport' in the German Press: An Analysis of Newspaper Discourse. *European Journal for Sport and Society, 18*(3), 265–282. 10.1080/16138171.2021.1930945

Michelini, E. (2021b). The Representation of Yusra Mardini as a Refugee Olympic Athlete: A Sociological Analysis. *Sport und Gesellschaft, 18*(1), 39–64. 10.1515/sug-2021-0003

Michelini, E. (2022). Organised Sport in Refugee Sites: An Ethnographic Research in Niamey. *European Journal for Sport and Society, 19*(1), 1–17. 10.1080/16138171.2021.1878433

Michelini, E., Bortoletto, N., & Porrovecchio, A. (2021). Outdoor Physical Activity during the Coronavirus Crisis. A Comparative Analysis of Governmental Restrictions related to the COVID-19 in Italy, France and Germany. *Frontiers in Public Health*. 10.3389/fpubh.2021.615745

Michelini, E., Bruland, J., & Janning, O. (2022). Biografien geflüchteter Leistungsfußballer: Eine sozialwissenschaftliche Analyse. http://hdl.handle.net/2003/40977

Michelini, E., & Burrmann, U. (2021). A Preliminary Impact Model for the Integration of Young Refugees through Sport Programmes. *CuSSoc, 6*(2), 265–281.

Michelini, E., Burrmann, U., Nobis, T., Tuchel, J., & Schlesinger, T. (2018). Sport Offers for Refugees in Germany. Promoting and Hindering Conditions in Voluntary Sport Clubs. *Society Register, 2*(1), 19–38. 10.14746/sr.2018.2.1.02

Michelini, E., Quade, S., Burrmann, U., & Neuber, N. (2021). Orientierung durch Sport – Evaluation von sportbezogenen Projekten für junge geflüchtete Menschen. In N. Neuber (Ed.), *Kinder- und Jugendsportforschung in Deutschland – Themen, Befunde, Transfer* (pp. 323–340). Wiesbaden: VS.

References 113

Michelini, E., & Schreiner, L. (2022-Submitted). Multiperspectivity in Organised Sport at Refugee Sites. Case Study-Based Sociological Findings and Pedagogical Considerations. *Frontiers in Sports and Active Living*.

Michelini, E., & Seiberth, K. (2022). Refugee, Footballer and (Anti-)Hero: The Case of Bakery Jatta. A Discourse Analysis of German Newspapers. *Soccer and Society*, Online first. 10.1080/14660970.2022.2080668

Middleton, T. R., Petersen, B., Schinke, R. J., & Giffin, C. (2020). Community Sport and Physical Activity Programs as Sites of Integration: A Meta-Synthesis of Qualitative Research Conducted with Forced Migrants. *Psychology of Sport and Exercise*, *51*, 101769. 10.1016/j.psychsport.2020.101769

Moeller, H. G. (2006). *Luhmann Explained: From Souls to Systems*. Chicago: Open Court.

Mohammadi, S. (2019). Social inclusion of newly arrived female asylum seekers and refugees through a community sport initiative: the case of Bike Bridge. *Sport in Society*, *22*(6), 1–25. 10.1080/17430437.2019.1565391

Moore, K., Berry, M., & Garcia-Blanco, I. (2018). Saving Refugees or Policing the Seas? How the national press of five EU member states framed news coverage of the migration crisis. *Justice, Power and Resistance*, *2*(1), 66–95.

Nagel, S. (2006). Mitgliederbindung in Sportvereinen-Ein akteurtheoretisches Analysemodell. [Commitment of Members in Sport Clubs-A Model Based on the General Theory of Action]. *Sport und Gesellschaft*, *3*(1), 33–56.

Nagel, S. (2007). Akteurtheoretische Analyse der Sportvereinsentwicklung. *German Journal of Exercise and Sport Research*, *37*(2), 186–201.

Nagel, S., Elmose-Østerlund, K., Zwahlen, J. A., & Schlesinger, T. (2020). Social Integration of People With a Migration Background in European Sports Clubs. *Sociology of Sport Journal*, *57*(4), 597–617. 10.1177/10126902211022921

Nagel, S., Schlesinger, T., Bayle, E., & Giauque, D. (2015). Professionalisation of sport federations–a multi-level framework for analysing forms, causes and consequences. *European Sport Management Quarterly*, *15*(4), 407–433. 10.1080/16184742.2015.1062990

Nassehi, A. (2005). Organizations as decision machines: Niklas Luhmann's theory of organized social systems. *Sociological Review Monograph*, *53*(2), 178–191. 10.1111/j.1467-954X.2005.00549.x

National Geographic Society. (1999). Europe. In National Geographic Society (Ed.), *National Geographic Atlas of the World* (7 ed., pp. 68–69). Washington, DC: National Geographic.

Nauright, J., Zipp, S., & Kim, Y. H. (2020). The sports world in the era of COVID-19. *Sport in Society*, *23*(11), 1703–1706. 10.1080/17430437.2020.1834196

Nobis, T. (2013). Multikulturelle Zivilgesellschaft? Sportverbände und -vereine als Akteure der Integrationsarbeit. In S. Braun (Ed.), *Der Deutsche Olympische Sportbund in der Zivilgesellschaft* (pp. 46–69). Wiesbaden: Springer.

Nobis, T. (2017). *Flüchtlingsarbeit von Sportvereinen – aüch für Mädchen und Fraüen? Konzepte, Maßnahmen und Perspektiven interkultureller Öffnüng von Sportvereinen* [Refugee Work for Sports Clubs - Also for Girls and Women? Concepts, Offers, and Perspectives of Intercultural Opening of Sports Clubs]. Berlin: Humboldt-University of Berlin.

114 References

Nobis, T., & Bauer, J. (Eds.). (2007). *Soziale Integration vereinsorganisierter Jugendlicher*. Köln: Strauß.

Noorden, D. (2014). Syrische topper in warm Emmens bad. *Dagblad Noorden*. https://www.dvhn.nl/archief/Syrische-topper-in-warm-Emmens-bad-20846939.html?harvest_referrer=https%3A%2F%2Fwww.google.com%2F

Nowy, T., Feiler, S., & Breuer, C. (2020). Investigating Grassroots Sports' Engagement for Refugees: Evidence From Voluntary Sports Clubs in Germany. *Journal of Sport and Social Issues*, *44*(1), 22–46. 10.1177/0193723519875889

Nyström, M., & Dahlberg, K. (2001). Pre-understanding and openness–a relationship without hope? *Scandinavian Journal of Caring Sciences*, *15*(4), 339–346.

O'Conner, J. (1981). The Meaning of Crisis. *International Journal of Urban & Regional Research*, *5*(3), 301–329. 10.1111/j.1468-2427.1981.tb00556.x

O'Driscoll, T., Banting, L. K., Borkoles, E., Eime, R., & Polman, R. (2014). A Systematic Literature Review of Sport and Physical Activity Participation in Culturally and Linguistically Diverse (CALD) Migrant Populations. *Journal of Immigrant and Minority Health*, *16*, 515–530. doi:0.1007/s10903-013-9857-x

Oberg, K. (2006). Cultural Shock: Adustement to New Cultural Environments. *curare*, *29*(2+3), 142–146.

Ochieng, P. (2009). An analysis of the strengths and limitation of qualitative and quantitative research paradigms. *Problems of Education in the 21st Century*, *13*, 13.

Paardekooper, B., De Jong, J., & Hermanns, J. (1999). The psychological impact of war and the refugee situation on South Sudanese children in refugee camps in Northern Uganda: an exploratory study. *Journal of child Psychology and Psychiatry*, *40*(4), 529–536.

Packer, M. J., & Addison, R. B. (1989). *Entering the circle: Hermeneutic investigation in psychology*. Albany: SUNY press.

Palliggiano, D. (2016). Gambia, la storia del Banjul United: il club dimezzato dalla povertà. *Corriere dello Sport*. https://www.corrieredellosport.it/news/calcio/calcio-estero/2016/11/30-18084643/gambia_la_storia_del_banjul_united_il_club_dimezzato_dalla_povert/

Parsons, T. (1951). *The Social System*. London: Routledge & Kegan.

Perry, M., Chase, M., Jacob, J., Jacob, M., & Daly, J. W. (2015). *Western Civilization: Ideas, Politics, and Society: Since 1400* (11 ed.). Boston: Cengage Learning.

Phillips, D. C. (1995). The good, the bad, and the ugly: The many faces of constructivism. *Educational researcher*, *24*(7), 5–12.

Pietilä, A. M., Hentinen, M., & Myhrman, A. (1995). The health behaviour of northern Finnish men in adolescence and adulthood. *International journal of nursing studies*, *32*(3), 325–338.

Pittaway, E., Bartolomei, L., & Hugman, R. (2010). 'Stop stealing our stories': The ethics of research with vulnerable groups. *Journal of human rights practice*, *2*(2), 229–251. 10.1093/jhuman/huq004

References 115

Potter, D., & Roksa, J. (2013). Accumulating advantages over time: Family experiences and social class inequality in academic achievement. *Social science research*, *42*(4), 1018–1032.

Pries, L. (2010). Soziologie der Migration [Migration Sociology]. In *Handbuch Spezielle Soziologien* (pp. 475–490). Wiesbaden: Springer.

Pyper, N. (2016). The murder of my friend Giulio Regeni in Egypt was an attack on academic freedom. *the Guardian*. https://www.theguardian.com/commentisfree/2016/feb/06/murder-giulio-regeni-egypt-academic-freedom-students

Rail, G., & Harvey, J. (1995). Body at work: Michel Foucault and the sociology of sport. *Sociology of Sport Journal*, *12*(2), 164–179.

Ramadan, A. (2013). Spatialising the Refugee Camp. *Transactions*, *38*(1), 65–77. 10.1111/j.1475-5661.2012.00509.x

Rand, E. (2012). *Red Nails, Black Skates: Gender, Cash, and Pleasure on and off the Ice*. Durham: Duke University Press.

Rankin, J. (2019). EU declares migration crisis over as it hits out at 'fake news'. *the Guardian*. https://www.theguardian.com/world/2019/mar/06/eu-declares-migration-crisis-over-hits-out-fake-news-european-commission

Reid, C., & Al Khalil, A. (2013). Refugee Cosmopolitans: Disrupting narratives of dependency. *Social Alternatives*, *32*(3), 14.

Rheindorf, M., & Wodak, R. (2018). Borders, Fences, and Limits—Protecting Austria From Refugees: Metadiscursive Negotiation of Meaning in the Current Refugee Crisis. *Journal of Immigrant & Refugee Studies*, *16*(1–2), 15–38. 10.1080/15562948.2017.1302032

Richardson, J. E. (2006). *Analysing Newspapers: An Approach from Critical Discourse Analysis*. New York: Palgrave Macmillan.

Rosa, H. (2003). Social Acceleration: Ethical and Political Consequences of a Desynchronized High-Speed Society. *Constellations*, *10*(1), 3–33.

Roth, S., & Schutz, A. (2015). Ten Systems: Toward a Canon of Function Systems. *Cybernetics & Human Knowing*, *22*(4), 11–31.

Roy, J., Singh, R., Roy, A., & Hamidan, S. (2012). Ramadan Fasting and Competitive Sports: Psychological Adaptation within Socio-Cultural Context. *International Journal of Psychological Studies*, *4*(4), 55–62. 10.5539/ijps.v4n4p55

Sandri, E. (2018). 'Volunteer Humanitarianism': Volunteers and Humanitarian Aid in the Jungle Refugee Camp of Calais. *Journal of Ethnic and Migration Studies*, *44*(1), 65–80. 10.1080/1369183X.2017.1352467

Schimank, U. (1988). Die Entwicklung des Sports zum gesellschaftlichen Teilsystem [The Development of Sport as a Social System]. In R. Mayntz (Ed.), *Differenzierung und Verselbständigung: Zur Entwicklung gesellschaftlicher Teilsysteme* (pp. 181–232). Frankfurt am Main: Campus.

Schimank, U. (2001). Die gesellschaftliche Entbehrlichkeit des Spitzensports und das Dopingproblem [The social dispensability of elite sport and the problem of doping]. In H. Digel (Ed.), *Spitzensport – Chancen und Probleme* (pp. 12–25). Schorndorf: Hofmann.

References

Schimank, U. (2008). Sport im Prozess gesellschaftlicher Differenzierung [Sports in the Process of Social Differentiation]. In K. Weis & A. Abraham (Eds.), *Handbuch Sportsoziologie* (pp. 68–74). Schorndorf: Hofmann.

Schinkel, W. (2018). Against 'Immigrant Integration': For an End to Neocolonial Knowledge Production. *Comparative Migration Studies*, *6*(1), 1–17. 10.1186/s40878-018-0095-1

Schirmer, W., & Michailakis, D. (2015). The Luhmannian Approach to Exclusion/Inclusion and its Relevance to Social Work. *Journal of Social Work*, *15*(1), 45–64. 10.1177/1468017313504607

Schmiedel, U., & Smith, G. (2018). *Religion in the European refugee crisis*. Wiesbaden: Springer.

Schneider, J., & Crul, M. (2010). New insights into assimilation and integration theory: Introduction to the special issue. *Ethnic and Racial Studies*, *33*(7), 1143–1148. 10.1080/01419871003777809

Schreier, M. (2014). Qualitative Content Analysis. In U. Flick (Ed.), *The SAGE Handbook of Qualitative Data Analysis* (pp. 170–183). London: SAGE.

Schütte, D. (2019). Die eigenen Verstrickungen reflektieren [Reflecting on Own Entanglements]. In M. E. Kaufmann, L. Otto, S. Nimführ, & D. Schütte (Eds.), *Forschen und Arbeiten im Kontext von Flucht: Reflexionslücken, Repräsentations- und Ethikfragen* (pp. 21–43). Wiesbaden: Springer.

Schütze, F. (1983). Biographieforschung und narratives Interview. [Biographic Research and Narrative Interview]. *Neue Praxis*, *13*(3), 283–293.

Schwanitz, D. (1995). Systems theory according to Niklas Luhmann: its environment and conceptual strategies. *Cultural Critique*, *30*(Spring), 137–170.

Scott, C.-G. (2015). *African Footballer in Sweden. Race, Immigration and Integration in the age of globalization*. New York: Palgrave and MacMillan.

Scott, W. R., & Davis, G. F. (2015). *Organizations and organizing: Rational, natural and open systems perspectives*. London and New York: Routledge.

Seiberth, K. (2010). *Fremdheit im Sport: ein theoretischer Entwurf; Erscheinungsformen, Erklärungsmodelle und pädagogische Implikationen*. Universitätsbibliothek Tübingen,

Seiberth, K. (2012). *Fremdheit im Sport: ein theoretischer Entwurf; Erscheinungsformen, Erklärungsmodelle und pädagogische Implikationen*. Hofmann: Schorndorf.

Seiberth, K., & Thiel, A. (2010). Cultural Diversity and Otherness in Sport–Prospect and Limits of Integration. In H. C. Traue, R. Johler, & J. J. Gavrilovic (Eds.), *Migration, Integration, and Health: The Danube Region* (pp. 189–203). Lengerich: Pabst Science.

Seiberth, K., & Thiel, A. (2014). Zum Topos des 'Interkulturellen' in interkulturell gekennzeichneten Konflikten im Sport. Eine konflikttheoretische Analyse. [The Topos of "Interculturality" in Interculturally Labelled Conflicts in Sport. A Conflict Theoretical Analysis]. *Sport und Gesellschaft*, *11*(1), 52–75.

References

Seiberth, K., Thiel, A., & Hanke, L. (2018). Flüchtlinge als neue Zielgruppe des organisierten Sports. Eine Pilot-Studie zur Entwicklung von Integrationsprojekten für Geflüchtete in Sportvereinen. [Refugees as a new Target Group for Organised Sport. A Pilot Study to Develop Integration Projects for Refugees in Sport Clubs]. *Z'Flucht, 2*(2), 262–291. 10.5771/25 09-9485-2018-2-262

Seiberth, K., Thiel, A., & Spaaij, R. (2017). Ethnic Identity and the Choice to Play for a National Team: A Study of Junior Elite Football Players with a Migrant Background. *Journal of Ethnic and Migration Studies, 45*(5), 787–803. 10.1080/1369183X.2017.1408460

Seiberth, K., Weigelt-Schlesinger, Y., & Schlesinger, T. (2013). Wie integrationsfähig sind Sportvereine?–Eine Analyse organisationaler Integrationsbarrieren am Beispiel von Mädchen und Frauen mit Migrationshintergrund. [What Is the Integrative Capacity of Sports Clubs?–An Analysis of Organizational Barriers to Integration based on the Example of Women and Girls with an Immigration Background]. *Sport und Gesellschaft, 10*(2), 174–198.

Seidl, D., & Becker, K. H. (2005). *Niklas Luhmann and organization studies*. Frederiksberg: CBS.

Seidl, D., & Schoeneborn, D. (2010). Niklas Luhmann's autopoietic theory of organisations: Contributions, limitations, and future prospects. *University of Zurich, Institute of Organization and Administrative Science*. http://papers.ssrn.com/sol3/papers.cfm?abstract_id=1552847#

Sigona, N. (2018). The Contested Politics of Naming in Europe's "Refugee Crisis". *Ethnic and Racial Studies, 41*(3), 456–460. 10.1080/01419870.2018. 1388423

Sironi, A., Bauloz, C., & Milen, E. (Eds.). (2019). *International Migration Law: Glossary on Migration*. Geneva: International Organization for Migration.

Smith-Spark, L. (2015). European migrant crisis: A country-by-country glance. *CNN*. http://edition.cnn.com/2015/09/04/europe/migrant-crisis-country-by-country/

Smith, R., Spaaij, R., & McDonald, B. (2019). Migrant Integration and Cultural Capital in the Context of Sport and Physical Activity: a Systematic Review. *Journal of international migration and integration, 20*, 851–868. 10. 1007/s12134-018-0634-5

Smith Tuhiwai, L. (1999). *Decolonizing Methodologies: Research and Indigenous Peoples*. London: Zed Books.

Spaaij, R., Broerse, J., Oxford, S., Luguetti, C., McLachlan, F., McDonald, B., ... Pankowiak, A. (2019). Sport, Refugees, and Forced Migration: A Critical Review of the Literature. *Frontiers in Sports and Active Living*. 10.3389/fspor.2019.00047

Spaaij, R., Luguetti, C., & De Martini Ugolotti, N. (2021). Forced migration and sport: an introduction. *Sport in Society, 25*(3), 405–417. 10.1080/17430437. 2022.2017616

118 References

Sparkes, A. C., & Stewart, C. (2016). Taking Sporting Autobiographies Seriously as an Analytical and Pedagogical Resource in Sport, Exercise and Health. *Qualitative Research in Sport, Exercise and Health*, *8*(2), 113–130. 10.1080/2159676X.2015.1121915

Spradley, J. P. (2016). *Participant Observation*. Long Grove: Waveland Press.

Startup, R. (1971). A Sociology of Migration? *The Sociological Quarterly*, *12*(2), 177–190.

Statista. (2020a). *Refugees and Asylum in Germany*. Hamburg: Statista.

Statista. (2020b). Überregionale Tageszeitungen. https://de.statista.com/statistik/studie/id/25727/dokument/ueberregionale-tageszeitungen-statista-dossier/

Stepputat, F., & Sørensen, N. N. (2014). Sociology and forced migration. In E. Fiddian-Qasmiyeh, G. Loescher, K. Long, & N. Sigona (Eds.), *The Oxford handbook of refugee and forced migration studies* (pp. 86–98). Oxford and New York: Oxford University Pres.

Stewart, E. (2008). Exploring the asylum-migration nexus in the context of health professional migration. *Geoforum*, *39*(1), 223–235. 10.1016/j.geoforum.2007.04.002

Stichweh, R. (1990). Sport-Ausdifferenzierung, Funktion, Code. [Sport Differentiation, Function, Code]. *Sportwissenschaft*, *20*(4), 373–389.

Stichweh, R. (2013). Sport as a Function System in World Society. *European Journal for Sport and Society*, *10*(2), 87–100.

Stichweh, R. (2018). *Sociocultural Evolution and Social Differentiation: The Study of the History of Society and the two Sociologies of Change and Transformation*. Academia, Preprint. https://www.academia.edu/27768612/Sociocultural_Evolution_and_Social_Differentiation_The_Study_of_the_History_of_Society_and_the_two_Sociologies_of_Change_and_Transformation_January_2018.

Stone, C. (2018). Utopian community football? Sport, hope and belongingness in the lives of refugees and asylum seekers. *Leisure Studies*, *37*(2), 171–183. 10.1080/02614367.2017.1329336

Straume, S., Bachmann, K., Skrove, G. K., Nærbøvik, S., & Røvik, K. (2018). Inclusion of refugees in Norwegian football clubs. *Working paper*. https://www.unit.no/ugyldig-lenke-til-dokument-i-vitenarkiv

Streule, R. (2020). Flüchtling und Topläufer: Wie Dominic Lobalu in St.Gallen für seine Karriere kämpft. *Tagblatt*. https://www.tagblatt.ch/sport/fluechtling-und-toplaeufer-wie-dominic-lobalu-in-stgallen-fuer-seine-karriere-kaempft-ld.1199982

Sukarieh, M., & Tannock, S. (2013). On the problem of over-researched communities: The case of the Shatila Palestinian refugee camp in Lebanon. *Sociology*, *47*(3), 494–508. 10.1177/0038038512448567

Tannen, D., Hamilton, H. E., & Schiffrin, D. (Eds.). (2015). *The Handbook of Discourse Analysis*. (2 ed.). West Sussex: Blackwell.

Telegraph, T. (2016). Gambia's Top Team Lose Half their Players as they Flee on People-Smuggling Boats to Europe. *The Telegraph*. https://www.

References 119

telegraph.co.uk/news/2016/11/30/gambias-top-teams-lose-half-players-flee-people-smuggling-boats/

Thangaraj, S. (2015). "They Said 'Go Back to Afghanistan'" South Asian American Basketball Culture and Challenging the "Terrorist" Stereotype. *Amerasia Journal*, *41*(2), 25–46. 10.17953/aj.41.2.25

Thiel, A., & Mayer, J. (2009). Characteristics of voluntary sports clubs management: A sociological perspective. *European Sport Management Quarterly*, *9*(1), 81–98. 10.1080/16184740802461744

Thiel, A., & Meier, H. (2004). Überleben durch Abwehr–Zur Lernfähigkeit des Sportvereins. [Survival through Resistance–About the Learning Capability of Sports Organizations]. *Sport und Gesellschaft*, *1*(2), 103–124.

Thiel, A., & Meier, H. (2008). Wie innovationsfähig ist der Sportverein? Eine Analyse am Beispiel der Einrichtung hauptberuflicher Mitarbeiterstellen. In M. K. W. Schweer (Ed.), *Sport in Deutschland. Bestandsaufnahmen und Perspektiven* (pp. 129–146). Frankfurt am Main: Lang.

Thiel, A., & Seiberth, K. (2020). Migration und Sport [Migration and Sport]. In A. Röder & D. Zifonun (Eds.), *Handbuch Migrationssoziologie* (pp. 1–24). Wiesbaden: VS.

Thiel, A., Seiberth, K., & Mayer, J. (2013). *Sportsoziologie. Ein Lehrbuch in 13 Lektionen* [Sociology of Sport. A Textbook in 13 Lessons]. Aachen: Meyer & Meyer.

Thiel, A., & Tangen, J. O. (2015). Niklas Luhmann, system theory and sport. In R. Giulianotti (Ed.), *Routledge handbook of the sociology of sport* (pp. 72–82). London and New York: Routledge.

Thompson, C. T., Vidgen, A., & Roberts, N. P. (2018). Psychological interventions for post-traumatic stress disorder in refugees and asylum seekers: A systematic review and meta-analysis. *Clinical Psychology Review*, *63*, 66–79. 10.1016/j.cpr.2018.06.006

Trainer 1. (2019) *Sport at the ETM of Niamey/Interviewer: E. Michelini*.

Trainer 2. (2019) *Sport at the ETM of Niamey/Interviewer: E. Michelini*.

Trainer 3. (2019) *Sport at the ETM of Niamey/Interviewer: E. Michelini*.

Trauner, F. (2016). Asylum policy: the EU's 'crises' and the looming policy regime failure. *Journal of European Integration*, *38*(3), 311–325. 10.1080/07036337.2016.1140756

Tuchel, J., Burrmann, U., Nobis, T., Michelini, E., & Schlesinger, T. (2021). Practices of Voluntary Sports Clubs to Include Refugees. *Sport in Society*, *24*(4), 670–692. 10.1080/17430437.2019.1706491

Tuck, E., & Yang, K. W. (2012). Decolonization is not a Metaphor. *Decolonization: Indigeneity, Education & Society*, *1*(1), 1–40.

Turner, S. (2016). What is a Refugee Camp? Explorations of the Limits and Effects of the Camp. *Journal of Refugee Studies*, *29*(2), 139–148. 10.1093/jrs/fev024

Tyrell, H. (1978). Anfragen an die Theorie der gesellschaftlichen Differenzierung. [Questions to the Theory of Social Differentiation]. *Zeitschrift für Soziologie*, *7*(2), 175–193.

120 References

Udehn, L. (2002). *Methodological individualism: Background, history and meaning.* London: Routledge.
UN. (1948). Universal Declaration of Human Rights. *UN General Assembly.* https://www.ohchr.org/EN/UDHR/Documents/UDHR_Translations/eng.pdf
UN. (2019). *Human Development Report.* New York: UN.
UNHCR. (2007). *Emergency Handbook* (3 ed.). Geneva: UNHCR.
UNHCR. (2010). *Convention and Protocol Relating to the Status of Refugees.* Geneva: UNHCR
UNHCR. (2019). Country Operation Update. http://reporting.unhcr.org/sites/default/files/UNHCR%20Niger%20Operational%20Update%20-%20May%202019.pdf
UNHCR. (2020a). Olympic Refuge Foundation: Sport can offer hope to displaced communities during the COVID-19 pandemic. https://www.unhcr.org/news/press/2020/5/5ec3f2e94/olympic-refuge-foundation-sport-offer-hope-displaced-communities-during.html
UNHCR. (2020b). Sport programmes and partnerships. http://www.unhcr.org/sport-partnerships.html?query=Sport
UNHCR. (2020c). What is a Refugee Camp? https://www.unrefugees.org/refugee-facts/camps/
UNHCR. (2021). Operational Portal: Refugee Situations. https://data2.unhcr.org/en/situations/mediterranean?page=1&view=grid&Type%255B%255D=3&Search=%2523monthly%2523
UNHCR. (2022a). Refugee Statistics. https://www.unhcr.org/refugee-statistics/download/?url=5ZNRgf
UNHCR. (2022b). Syria emergency. https://www.unhcr.org/syria-emergency.html#:~:text=Millions%20of%20Syrians%20have%20escaped,currently%20more%20than%203.6%20million
UNHCR. (2022c). Ukraine Refugee Situation. https://data2.unhcr.org/en/situations/ukraine
UNHCR, International Olympic Committee, & Terre des hommes. (2018). *Sport for Protection Toolkit: Programming with Young People in Forced Displacement Settings.* Geneva: UNHCR.
Verweyen, L. (2019). Ankommen im Sport: Integrationsarbeit mit Geflüchteten und der Beitrag der Ethnologie [Welcome in Sport: Integration Work with Refugees and the Contribution of Ethnology]. In S. Klocke-Daffa (Ed.), *Angewandte Ethnologie: Perspektiven einer anwendungsorientierten Wissenschaft* (pp. 559–575). Wiesbaden: Springer.
Vollmer, B., & Karakayali, S. (2018). The Volatility of the Discourse on Refugees in Germany. *Journal of Immigrant & Refugee Studies, 16*(1–2), 118–139. 10.1080/15562948.2017.1288284
Von Glasersfeld, E. (1995). *Radical Constructivism.* London: Falmer.
Waardenburg, M., Visschers, M., Deelen, I., & Liempt, I. V. (2018). Sport in liminal spaces: The meaning of sport activities for refugees living in a

References 121

reception centre. *International Review for the Sociology of Sport*, *54*(8), 938–956. 10.1177/1012690218768200

Wacquant, L. J. (1995). Pugs at work: Bodily capital and bodily labour among professional boxers. *Body & Society*, *1*(1), 65–93.

Waddington, I., Malcolm, D., & Green, K. (1997). Sport, Health and Physical Education: A Reconsideration. *European Physical Education Review*, *3*(2), 165–182.

Weber, B. (2016). "We Must Talk about Cologne": Race, Gender, and Reconfigurations of "Europe". *German Politics and Society*, *34*(4), 68–86. 10.3167/gps.2016.340405

Weckelman, J. (2018). Linkshänder aus Syrien [Left-Handed from Syria]. *Westfale*. https://issuu.com/janweckelmann/docs/westfale2018_1_web

Weesjes, E. (2016). Timeline Refugee Crisis. *Natural Hazards Observer*. https://hazards.colorado.edu/article/timeline-refugee-crisis-from-may-2011-february-2016

West, C., & Zimmerman, D. H. (1987). Doing Gender. *Gender & Society*, *1*(2), 125–151.

Whannel, G. (2013). Reflections on communication and sport: On mediatization and cultural analysis. *Communication & Sport*, *1*(1–2), 7–17. 10.1177/2167479512471335

Willimczik, K. (2007). Die Vielfalt des Sports. *Sportwissenschaft*, *37*(1), 19–37.

Willke, H. (2006). *Grundlagen: eine Einführung in die Grundprobleme der Theorie sozialer Systeme* [Systems Theory: Foundations: An Introduction to the Basic Problems of the Theory of Social Systems] (7 ed.). Stuttgart: Lucius & Lucius.

Willke, H. (2007). *Smart Governance: Governing the Global Knowledge Society*. Frankfurt: Campus.

Witten, I. H., Bainbridge, D., & Nichols, D. M. (2010). *How to Build a Digital Library*. Burlington: Elsevier.

Wodak, R., & Meyer, M. (Eds.). (2001). *Methods of Critical Discourse Analysis*. London, Thousand Oaks, New Dehli: SAGE.

Wright Mills, C. (2000). *The Sociological Imagination* (3rd ed.). Oxford: Oxford University Press.

Yakushko, O., Watson, M., & Thompson, S. (2008). Stress and Coping in the Lives of Recent Immigrants and Refugees: Considerations for Counseling. *International Journal for the Advancement of Counselling*, *30*(3), 167–178. 10.1007/s10447-008-9054-0

Zender, U. (2018). *Sportengagements türkisch-muslimischer Migrantinnen. Der Einfluss von Kultur, Religion und Herkunftsfamilie* [Sport Engagements of Turkish-Muslim Migrants. The Influence of Culture, Religion and Family of Origin]. Wiesbaden: Springer.

Zick, A., Pettigrew, T. F., & Wagner, U. (2008). Ethnic Prejudice and Discrimination in Europe. *Journal of Social Issues*, *64*(2), 233–251.

Index

Note: **Bold** page numbers refer to tables and *italic* page numbers refer to figures.

Activities for Refugees in Sports Clubs project 13, 35, **40**, **51**, 54–58, 68, **74**
Agamben, G. xiv, 32, 84
Agergaard, S. 12
amateur sport in refugee crisis 33, 81–83
asylum migration 16, 80
autopoietic social systems 35

Bauer, J. 12
Bertalanffy, L. V. 38n1
Bette, K.-H. 34
Biggs, D. 18
Bradley, J. 86
Braun, S. 10, 12
Brunner, O. 17
Burrmann, U. 12

capacity drain 9
Caudwell, J. xii
cause-effect relationship 29
Clarke, V. 12
crisis 31; Luhmann's analysis of 31; and migration crises 17–19; as a self-fulfilling prophecy 32
critical theory 18

dependency syndrome 84
discourse 37
displaced persons 14–16
document analysis 39

economic migration 16
elite sport 33, 79–81

Emergency Transit Mechanism of Niamey 45, 58–59
Esser, H. 8
European refugee crisis xii–xiii; between 2015 and 2016 24; timeline of 21, *22*
EU-Turkey Deal 25
exercise and sport 16–17

Farah, M. 63
Finke, S. 10
Forced Migration and Elite Sport project **28**, 36, **40**, **47**, **51**, 62–70, **74**, 88, 90
forced migration and sport 3, 5–13, 14–19; critical review of the literature 12–13; distribution of articles on *41*, *42*; elite sport and 36, 62–66; key terms in, definitions 14–19; in the mass media 34; neighbouring disciplines and research areas 7–10; political discourse and 9; qualitative research studies 11; sociology of migration 7; sociology of sport 7; special sociologies 7; state of the art research on 7–13
forced migration in mass media 50–54
Foucault, M. 92
future perspectives 88–92
future scientific agenda 90

Georgiou, M. 21

Index 123

habilitation, methodological approaches of 39, **40**
Heinemann, K. 17
holistic considerations of research 73–76; inclusion at elite and amateur level 73; individual biographies and sport organisations, comparison 75; motivation and sacrifice 75
Hurrelmann, K. 37

integration 7
interaction 30
intersectionality 85
Italy and Libya, bilateral agreement between 25
irritation 25, 32, 54

Jatta, B. 1, **51**, 70, 79; Koselleck, R. 18, 64

Kurdi, A. 25

leisure sport 33, 83–84
Lomong, L. 63
Luhmann, N. 27, 29, 31, 35, 64; Luhmann's systems theory 27

Mardini, Y. 48n2, **51**, 70; ...
mass media, researching 41–43
methodical approaches of the projects 39–48; data collection 47; habilitation 39, **40**; interviews in sports clubs 43, **44**; relevant articles 41, *42*; researching mass media 41–43; researching refugee athletes 46–48; researching refugee sites 44–46; researching sport organisations 43–44
Middleton, T. R. 11
migrants 14–16; asylum migration 16; economic migration 16; typology of 15, *15*
migration and sport 8–9; crises 17–19; in-depth theorisations of 18; *see also* forced migration and sport
Mills, C. W. 63

Niamey's refugee sites 45, **45**
Nobis, T. 10, 12

organisations 30
Orientation through Sport (OtS) 43, 54

peak phase of refugee crisis 24, 79, 81
physical activity (PA): exercise, sport and 16–17; in refugee sites 36, 58–62
Physical Activity in Refugee Sites project 36, 40, **51**, 58–62, 68–69, **74**, 88, 90
post-peak phase of refugee crisis 24, 79, 82
post-structuralism 37
pre-peak phase of refugee crisis 24, 79
projects results 50–66; *Activities for Refugees in Sports Clubs* 50, **51**, 54–58; athletes 53; criminality 53; engagement 53; *Forced Migration and Elite Sport* 50, **51**; forced migration and elite sport 62–66; housing 53; integration 53; *Physical Activity in Refugee Sites* 50, **51**, 58–62; 'quantitative' information 52; resources 53; *Sport and Forced Migration in the Mass Media* 50, **51**, 68–70

qualitative research, influencing factors 86

refugee 14–16; sports clubs, activities for 54–58
refugee athletes, representations of 68–71; organisations and sport activities for refugees 71–73; researching 46–48; in sports clubs and refugee sites 71, **72**; *see also* holistic considerations of research
refugee crisis xiv, 20–26; context of 20–23; European 'refugee crisis', timeline of 21, *22*; long summer of migration 25; peak (2015–2016) phase 24; post-peak (2017–2018) phase 24; pre-peak (2013–2014) phase 24; as a process 24–25; sport in 26; on sports clubs, impact of 54, 55
refugee crisis, role of sport within 78–84; call to scientific community

124 *Index*

91–92; elite sport 79–81; leisure sport 83–84; limitations 85–88; methodological aspects 86–87; practical aspects 87–88
refugee sites: physical activity in 36; researching 44–46
refugee-specific sport programmes 54, **56**
research gaps 88–90; in existing systematic review analyses 89; lack of sociological perspective 89; scientific staff with a refugee background 89
research projects: and scientific articles 50, **51**; types of systems and 68, *69*
researching mass media 41–43
Richter, M. W. 18
Russia-Ukraine war xii
Ryba, T. V. 12

Seiberth, K. 12
self-referential systems 30
socialisation theory 37
societies 30
sociology of migration 7
sociology of sport 7
Spaaij, R. xii, 86
Sport and Forced Migration in the Mass Media project 34–35, **40**, **51**, 68–70, **74**

sport and refugee crisis 2–4; research question 4–5; as a research topic 2–4; structure 5–6
sport and society, reciprocal influences between 8
Sport for Development and Peace (SFDP) 59
sport in the 'refugee crisis' 26
sports clubs 35, 82
Stichweh, R. 33
Syrian Civil War 1, 24
systems theory 18, 27–36; general assumptions 28–30; interaction 30; irritation 32; Luhmann's systems theory 27, 29, 31; organisations 30; self-referential systems 30; societies in 30; specific concepts 30–34; sport system 33; theoretical framework 27–38; typification of the considered systems 34–36

Thiel, A. 12
typology of systems 29, *29*

Ukrainian refugee crisis xiv
United Nations High Commissioner for Refugees 59

Zaborowski, R. 21
Zimmerman, D. H. 92n3